Every D[...]

JUL/AUG 2021

WAVERLEY ABBEY
RESOURCES

MIX
Paper from
responsible sources
www.fsc.org   FSC® C021017

Deuteronomy 34
**'Now Joshua son of Nun was filled with the spirit of wisdom
because Moses had laid his hands on him. So the Israelites
listened to him and did what the LORD had commanded Moses.'** (v9)

Thresholds are liminal spaces: a boundary between two points
in time, space, or both. All thresholds offer both a risk and an
opportunity. Joshua, anointed through the laying on of Moses'
hands, is appointed as God's man to lead Israel across the Jordan into
the Promised Land, a threshold of momentous proportions.

We live in a world we might describe as 'drowning in words'. Social
media platforms multiply and news sources are birthed daily. How
can we discern what is true from what isn't? Whilst the first known
use of the phrase, 'fake news', occurred in the 1890s, it was only in
2016 that Buzzfeed's media editor, Craig Silverman, noticed a funny
stream of completely made-up stories apparently originating from one
small Eastern European town.

I say this simply to establish that it's essential we learn to choose
carefully who and what we believe. We need to discern truth from
error. One guiding principle Jesus has given us is the fruit of a
person's life. Does this fruit reveal Christlike values (Matt. 5:15–20)?

The importance of accurate information and remaining Christ-
centred cannot be overemphasised. Rumours spread like wildfire,
creating panic and confusion, as Moses discovered.

RELATED SCRIPTURE TO CONSIDER: Exod. 15:22–27; 32:1–8; 1 Tim. 3:1–12;
Titus 1:5–16.

AN ACTION TO TAKE: How do you decide what and who you can trust from across
the many media platforms you might consult today?

A PRAYER TO MAKE: 'Lord, please speak to me through Your Word so that I might
follow You faithfully. Amen.'

Write to **micha@edwj.org** and I'll write back personally and in confidence as
soon as I can.

Psalm 105
**'Look to the LORD and his strength; seek his face always.
Remember the wonders he has done, his miracles,
and the judgments he pronounced.'** (vv4–5)

We build out of who we are. The danger in a world consumed with watching others is that we seek to fashion ourselves in the image of another. All-embracing globalisation creates a manufactured culture that threatens to diminish, if not eradicate, all others. The familiarity of Coca Cola serves as a useful example. First sold in 1886, it has a company mission to sell the largest number of beverages to the greatest number of people. Its logo is instantly identifiable and Coke created our modern Santa!

God through Scripture reminds His disciples that they're a product of a long, eventful history. A people who've navigated many cultures and social conditions, yet retained the faith of their forebears. Indeed, if we want to know who we are and what God requires of us, we have only to turn to God's Word. We discover generations of God's followers intent on obeying God within challenging, often alien, contexts.

Family reputation is important to God. Our acknowledgement and representation of the family business loving God and neighbour is critical for reflecting what is truly our international identity. It's called the kingdom of God, ushered in by Jesus, and it is our responsibility to curate and extend it as those who've bowed the knee in allegiance to God. Christianity truly is a global brand.

RELATED SCRIPTURE TO CONSIDER: Jer. 17:5–10; Amos 5:4–15; Gal. 3:23–29; Col. 2:6–15.

AN ACTION TO TAKE: Where do you take your guidance from, and whose interests do you represent with your life choices?

A PRAYER TO MAKE: 'Lord, help me to discern and to live Your way in this world, and not to be swayed by life's many distractions. Amen.'

Psalm 1

**'Blessed is the one who does not walk in step with the wicked
or stand in the way that sinners take or sit in the company
of mockers, but whose delight is in the law of the LORD,
and who meditates on his law day and night.'** (vv1–2)

God's Word introduces us to God's way. It is not one we naturally
aspire to. It requires that we both submit to God and serve
others. In our material world, in which purpose has been
reduced to serving personal interests, wickedness too often triumphs.
When I put myself first, God's ignored and others suffer. No surprises,
for we know the human heart is desperately wicked (Jer. 17:9). When
serving my interests, wickedness too often triumphs.

If our natural inclination is towards evil, doing the wrong thing, it
stands to reason that it will demand some effort to do the right thing.
However, history reveals that the best of human intention has failed to
turn a fallen world right side up. Therefore, the effort required is not
what we do, but who we serve.

I can never walk in the ways of God until I fully surrender to serve
God and God's global purpose. This will require that I set aside
personal ambition in preference for serving God. Simply said, my
experience is that this is the battle of a lifetime. As someone once
said, when Paul tells us to offer ourselves as a living sacrifice
(Rom. 12:1), our natural inclination is to seek escape by continually
attempting to crawl off God's altar and take back control of our lives:
one reason we choose to read *EDWJ* and seek our nourishment within
God's Word, both day and night.

RELATED SCRIPTURE TO CONSIDER: Psa. 51; 1 Sam. 12:6–25; Rom. 3:9–31; 12:1–8.

AN ACTION TO TAKE: What is the biggest battle you have with putting God's will
and purpose first in your life?

A PRAYER TO MAKE: 'Lord "All to Jesus I surrender, I surrender all"'. May I
remember to surrender every moment of everyday. Amen.'

*Lyrics, Judson W. Van de Venter (1855–1939); music, Winfield Scott Weeden (1847–1908))

Colossians 3

'Since, then, you have been raised with Christ, set your hearts on things above, where Christ is, seated at the right hand of God. Set your minds on things above, not on earthly things.' (vv1–2)

Following Jesus begins with a decision. At some point we must say yes, or no, to God. We don't stumble into God's kingdom. No one gets married unintentionally. Indeed, there's often months of preparation before couples make their decision publicly. As Christians we are the Bride of Christ (Rev. 21:9), so we are to live true to our vows of commitment to Jesus.

As with marriage, following Jesus demands we leave one way of life to embrace another. No longer totally alone, we need to learn to live in close proximity with another; in this case, the Holy Spirit. Whatever our status in life single, married, divorced or widowed we are, once with Christ, never alone. This means our thoughts and actions are always available to God for scrutiny. We may be able to deceive ourselves and others, but never God.

So, we must set our minds to living God's way as revealed in Scripture. It's one measure of our determination. There are many hazards along the way, but determination, a willingness to keep trying, is the true measure of our Christian commitment. On reflection I can point to innumerable personal failures but, upon confession, I find forgiveness. I pick myself up to resume my journey. God's Word encourages us to keep pursuing our desire to walk in Jesus' footsteps.

RELATED SCRIPTURE TO CONSIDER: Deut. 6:1–9; Psa. 103; Rom. 14:1–12; 1 John 1:5–10.

AN ACTION TO TAKE: What undermines your determination to walk in Jesus' footsteps?

A PRAYER TO MAKE: 'Lord, help me to choose to serve You every day, in my thoughts, words and deeds. Amen.'

2 Corinthians 5:18–21
'We are therefore Christ's ambassadors, as though God were making his appeal through us. We implore you on Christ's behalf: be reconciled to God.' (v20)

Christopher Meyer, UK American Ambassador 1997–2003, describing his role, wrote, 'You must be able to negotiate, to win the confidence of the powerful and influence them, to understand what makes a foreign society tick, to analyse information and report it accurately and quickly, including what your own government does not want to hear; you need a quick mind, a hard head, a strong stomach, a warm smile and a cold eye'.*

As Christ's ambassadors, is our role similar? We must negotiate and make our case to the powerful few, whose decisions influence the lives of millions. Scripture illustrates this in the contribution of the prophets in the Old Testament and apostles in the New. We can't assume society will continue as before, for society is consistently challenged and changed by new ideas.

Whilst God rules supreme, and the end of all things is secured through Christ's victory, we, as citizens of heaven, have a responsibility to represent God's interests. To do this we must first understand the society in which we live as exiles, and prayerfully analyse all we observe, weighing the results against Scripture and Christian tradition.

As Meyer points out, it must involve our whole character; and whilst we needn't report to an all-knowing government what they don't want to hear, we must pray for wisdom and grace to represent God's Word to God's world effectively.

RELATED SCRIPTURE TO CONSIDER: Ezek. 33:1–20; Acts 16:16–40; Phil. 3:15–4:1; 1 Pet. 2:9–17.

AN ACTION TO TAKE: What steps can you take to best represent your heavenly citizenship in your life?

A PRAYER TO MAKE: 'Lord, may I daily represent the values and interests of God's kingdom. Amen.'

*Christopher Meyer *DC Confidential*, (London: Weidenfeld & Nicolson, 2011)

The Big Bounce Forwards
The Big Church Read

Bouncing Forwards by Patrick Regan has been chosen for the Big Church Read. Here's what you need to know. The Big Church read is all about journeying through the book with the author, and then meeting in-person or online to talk about what they have read.

After a tough year for the Church, Waverley Abbey Resources are proud to be supporting this fantastic initiative, and we're so pleased that *Bouncing Forwards* has been selected for it. From 8 September, each Wednesday morning for 10 weeks the Big Church Read will release weekly exclusive videos and content from Patrick Regan to enhance your reading experience.

About Bouncing Forwards

We've all faced difficulties over the last year in some shape or form. Often when we go through challenging times, we're told, 'You'll bounce back.' As well-meant as these words area, the tough times we've been through leave us scarred and changed – so why would we want to go back when we've learnt so much? It's time to bounce *forwards* instead.

In *Bouncing Forwards*, Patrick draws on his own journey of making peace with his on-going anxiety, to look honestly and vulnerably at the temptation to wait for the day when all will be well whilst missing out on what's happening in the here and now. Exploring resilience, acceptance and emotional agility, Patrick shows how we can find meaning in some of life's toughest moments and the hope to journey on.

To find out more about Bouncing Forwards and the Big Church Read, and to make use of the **bulk-buy discount**, visit **waverleyabbeyresources.org/bf**

God's Kingdom

Colossians 1:9–14

'so that you may live a life worthy of the LORD and please him in every way: bearing fruit in every good work, growing in the knowledge of God' (v10)

If we are to represent God effectively, we must first comprehend what God requires. From the point of conversion we start a journey of internal change that influences external behaviour. At the point of my conversion I did not lose my 'old life' overnight. I had a new allegiance to Jesus, but I was a 'baby Christian'. I didn't have the wisdom I've painfully, and at times reluctantly, accumulated through life experience.

Friendship with God, like all relationships, is organic. No one sincerely embracing Christ immediately breaks with their past. Yes, some aspects from our previous way of life may fall away suddenly; these are the first fruits confirming that a new relationship has been born. A friend of mine cycling to school, post conversion, was surrounded in the playground on arrival and asked what had happened to her? Enquiring what they meant, they said she hadn't sworn once, something most out of character for her. Sadly, that was not my experience.

God invites us to take time building our friendship with Him so that we produce the fruit of the Christian life. We have a responsibility to clothe ourselves in God's Word so that God's truth is evidenced through our lives. One reason we take time with God every day is so that we can live just such a fruitful and productive life, serving God.

RELATED SCRIPTURE TO CONSIDER: Exod. 20; Rom. 8:1–17; 13:8–14; Col. 3:5–17.

AN ACTION TO TAKE: How are you viewed by family, friends and colleagues? Are there useful adjustments you could make to help them encounter Jesus?

A PRAYER TO MAKE: 'Lord, accompany me on my journey as I seek to grow in Christian maturity and become more like Jesus every day. Amen.'

Philippians. 3:15–21
**'But our citizenship is in heaven. And we eagerly await
a Saviour from there, the LORD Jesus Christ.'** (v20)

C hristianity is future proofed. History will end with Christ's return.
If we don't believe that, then the whole message of redemption
unravels. We are also encouraged that mortality is merely a brief
delay to immortality with God.

It was Francis of Assisi who commanded death to do its work as
God's slave and carry his ailing body into God's presence. Death is not
to be feared for Christ has conquered death, which now serves one
purpose only; to carry God's followers into God's embrace.

Even greater news! God's kingdom begins even this side of death.
Filled with God's Spirit, we can live as citizens of heaven, our true
nationality from the moment we choose God. The Holy Spirit is our
passport and we enthusiastically demonstrate the culture of our
homeland to which we shall eventually return. As exiles, displaced
people in time and space, we invest all our energy introducing the
earthbound to the possibilities of an unseen yet practical life of hope,
regardless of the realities presented by our mortal existence.

It has been said of Christians that they are too heavenly minded to
be of any earthly use. I say, until we are heavenly minded we cannot
be of any earthly use. We live as advocates and guides to a kingdom
built upon faith, hope and love.

RELATED SCRIPTURE TO CONSIDER: Isa. 25:1–9; 1 Cor. 13; 15; 2 Cor. 5:1–10.

AN ACTION TO TAKE: How does imagining heaven influence the life decisions you take?

A PRAYER TO MAKE: 'Lord, help to live with my heart in God's heaven, and my feet on earth. Amen.'

Ephesians. 2:19–22
**'Consequently, you are no longer foreigners and
strangers, but fellow citizens with God's people
and also members of his household'** (v19)

It might appear that this scripture is answering the question about
who I am. Yet, questions of identity offer us little hope of validation
or encouragement. This verse is more about where I find myself,
an issue of location rather than status. Society too often demands I
define myself by status my job title, for instance and itself seeks to
define me within predetermined sociological constraints.

The Bible defines us according to our relationship with God. Either
we are within God's kingdom, or outside it. Locations are easier to
establish than identities. So I have the privilege of choosing to enter
into a relationship with God and move from a finite to an infinite
geography. In this way of thinking, every decision I take will have
eternal consequences.

I remember as a youth, my first thought was always about my own
safety. I lied about and manipulated my circumstances to avoid my
wrongdoing being discovered. But Jesus knew all that about me
before he offered me residence within his 'household'. Once there, I
found I had less to worry about concerning my status this is forever
guaranteed in Christ than in my willingness to embrace and live God's
way, which means owning my wrongdoing and seeking to live by
God's kingdom patterns for all of life.

RELATED SCRIPTURE TO CONSIDER: Gen. 3:8–11; Jonah 1:1–12; Gal. 6:1–10;
Eph. 2:1–18.

AN ACTION TO TAKE: Stop worrying about who you are, and start deciding where
you are and where you want to get to?

A PRAYER TO MAKE: 'Lord, let me live within the household of faith and live a
kingdom life as a citizen of heaven. Amen.'

Animosity

John 15:18–25
'If you belonged to the world, it would love you as its own. As it is, you do not belong to the world, but I have chosen you out of the world. That is why the world hates you.' (v19)

I became a Christian at university. From a non-Christian family, I encountered Christ and began to learn to walk God's way; a challenge for any teenager. Every Thursday afternoon someone came round to lead me in a new believer's Bible study. On one occasion, there was a knock at my door. It opened and an old school friend looked in. His cheerful smile turned to a quizzical look as he asked, 'What are you doing?' 'I've become a Christian and I'm having a Bible study'. Instantly, with some very unparliamentary language, he turned on his heel declaring me to be a loser. I have never seen him again to this day.

Changing location changes perception: my own and those of others towards me. For five years my dad and I hardly spoke because he was so disappointed that I 'threw' my work opportunities away to serve Jesus. As a youth worker I also met with many parents who warned me off motivating their children to serve in mission.

Today, Christians are often intensely disliked. Their faith scorned and their contribution to public debate derided and mocked. Yet, no surprise. Jesus said it would be like this. Our challenge is to keep living as citizens of heaven rather than being intimidated and conforming to this world.

RELATED SCRIPTURE TO CONSIDER: Lev. 26: 14–46; Psa. 119:105–112; John 17:6–23; 1 John 4:1–6.

AN ACTION TO TAKE: Scripture ensures we know how we are to live as citizens of heaven. I recommend Search the Scriptures, an excellent three-year course to teach us how we should live; visit **edwj.org/ja21-9jul**

A PRAYER TO MAKE: 'Lord, help me always to refuse to be conformed to this world, rather seeking to be transformed through the renewing of my mind, by Your Word. Amen.'

Matthew 5:13–16

'In the same way, let your light shine before others, that they may see your good deeds and glorify your Father in heaven.' (v16)

Teresa of Avila wrote in the sixteenth century, 'Christ has no body now, but yours. No hands, no feet on earth but yours... Yours are the hands, yours are the feet, yours are the eyes, you are his body. Christ has no body now on earth but yours.'[']

Whatever our location, our actions speak loudly of who we are and the values we pursue. What we discover in God's Word often flies in the face of basic human instinct. When a young Christian, the meaning of J.O.Y. was explained as putting Jesus first, Yourself last and Others in between. God invites us to approach life differently to the common wisdom generated from within a secular and material world.

God's invitation is for us to live every day as Christ's ambassadors. The validity of Jesus is measured by others observing how we approach life; the good and the bad times. When plunged into the role of carer for my first wife, I was unprepared and I found it an unwelcome interruption in our life plan. Could I find Jesus within it? Was I willing to search for J.O.Y. in my own anger and confusion?

It is always less about what I say I believe, and everything to do with how what I say I believe shapes my perspective on life and my activities throughout my lifetime. It's the essence of our responsibility in representing God's truth to a fallen world.

RELATED SCRIPTURE TO CONSIDER: Prov. 6:20–24; Isa. 42:1–9; John 8:12–20; 9:1–5.

AN ACTION TO TAKE: Reflect upon your motivations across the different aspects of your life. Are they built upon J.O.Y?

A PRAYER TO MAKE: 'Lord, I dedicate my hands, my feet and my eyes to You. May I live to do Your will and reveal the character of God's kingdom in all things. Amen.'

Write to **micha@edwj.org** and I'll write back personally and in confidence as soon as I can.

'journeywithjesus.net/PoemsAndPrayers/Teresa_Of_Avila_Christ_Has_No_Body.shtml [accessed 22/04/2021]

2 Peter 3:8–13

'But in keeping with his promise we are looking forward to a new heaven and a new earth, where righteousness dwells.' (v13)

When I struggle with something, one major challenge is to keep things in perspective. In all the psychometric tests my character traits reveal I quickly move from calm to storm, and tend to catastrophize my future. It has taken time to learn not to gaze at a half empty, but rather a half full glass. Indeed, perhaps I should really learn to live with a glass that runs over with God's grace, regardless of circumstance (Psa. 23:5). We are all on a learning adventure; it's called spiritual formation.

One reason my cup's half empty is my failure fully to surrender my life to God's care. I feel compelled to take some responsibility for my present and my future. Jesus points out that each day has enough troubles of its own. I discovered that I could easily miss today, consumed only with my tomorrows yet to come.

It's healthy to pause and reflect regularly on the fact that, just as I can't add a single hour to my life (Psa. 139:16), I can, with confidence, serve and celebrate God in the present moment. For we all want friends and family to be present with us, a presence too often stolen by the relentless demands of our social media feeds. We each serve at the pleasure of the Lord who alone shapes the direction of our life.

RELATED SCRIPTURE TO CONSIDER: Psa. 23; 139; Isa. 40:21–31; Matt. 6:19–27.

AN ACTION TO TAKE: Are you comfortable entrusting all of your life to God? Where are the sticking points? Talk to God, and close friends, about these and find God's way forward for you.

A PRAYER TO MAKE: 'Lord, help me to build my confidence in Your total care and provision for all of my life. Amen.'

2 Timothy 3:10–17
'All Scripture is God-breathed and is useful for teaching, rebuking, correcting and training in righteousness.' (v16)

Since writing *EDWJ*, I've received a lot of feedback. The change was always going to be difficult for some. I've also received useful requests, such as a larger font and more related scriptures to study each day. However, one thing remains true: the Word of God is central to how we encounter God and live the Christian life.

Paul declares that Scripture is 'God-breathed' (Gen. 2:7). The same breath that gave life to the first mortals, themselves shaped by God, is the breath that informed the many who contributed to the Scriptures we study so carefully today.

They remain the source of informed, life-giving counsel by which we order our ways in every sphere of life. This is why we take them so seriously. They lay the foundations that encourage us all to live every day with Jesus. There is no alternate source for God's truth. Hence, we handle it carefully. We can also approach in a number of different ways, and each of us might have a preference in how we engage with Scripture, but let's recognise that God speaks in many and various ways (Heb. 1:1).

The baseline is this: if we want to encounter God, then it is to the Bible we turn. This is the book of life in which we can encounter Jesus, Himself described as the Word of life.

RELATED SCRIPTURE TO CONSIDER: Josh. 1:7–9; Psa. 119:9–16; John 1:1–5; 1 John 1:1–4.

AN ACTION TO TAKE: Do you take time reading Scripture every day? Try setting 15 minutes aside daily to read the Bible.

A PRAYER TO MAKE: 'Lord, may I read the Word of God in Scripture and meditate on it day and night, and be careful to do everything written in it. Amen' (cf Josh. 1:8).

James 1:19–27

'But whoever looks intently into the perfect law that gives freedom and continues in it – not forgetting what they have heard but doing it – they will be blessed in what they do.' (v25)

The Bible is a down to earth and practical guide to living the Christian life. It serves as our ambassador's handbook, as we represent God's interests in a world that has all but lost sight of God. Knowing Scripture is only useful in as far as it redirects our steps to follow closely in those of Jesus.

Many of my preconceptions about life, forged through family and education, have come up short when confronted by Scripture. I recall my mum constantly advising me not to stick my neck out. Her preferred illustration, the tortoise. It withdraws its vulnerable head and neck within a defensive shell. But, as I reminded her, the tortoise makes no progress unless and until it sticks its neck out.

Scripture invites us to stick our neck out. We are not to be dictated to by peer pressure or social norms. God has one clear purpose; to make Jesus' name known to the farthest parts of the globe (Matt. 28:19–20). The risk is all part of our adventure in serving God.

To follow Scripture's instruction may mean some spring cleaning as we reorder our lives so that they can reflect God's Bible truths. Bottom line, to know about God without living like Jesus is not to embrace the challenge to be a contemporary disciple. This requires courage and conviction, both of which are found in spades within the pages of the Bible.

RELATED SCRIPTURE TO CONSIDER: Psa. 119:129–136; Prov. 2; Matt. 4:1–4; 7:21–29.

AN ACTION TO TAKE: Take time with your Ambassador's handbook and determine how you can best represent God's interests to everyone you meet today, and every day.

A PRAYER TO MAKE: 'Lord, help me to take a risk in living God's way and representing God's interests everywhere I go. Amen.'

Psalm 1:1–3
**'but whose delight is in the law of the LORD, and
who meditates on his law day and night.'** (v2)

Scripture offers a variety of ways by which the disciple might encounter God. One way is to take time to meditate upon its content. I received some correspondence asking why it is that I keep us all in one short passage over a number of days? The reason is that we might contemplate what God is saying deeply. This is meditation.

Some fear meditation, assuming it is an eastern religious practice. This is not what is meant here by the psalmist. Meditation actually means to think something over carefully, to seriously consider. Given the seriousness of our subject matter and the potential for good that lies within each word, it certainly deserves deep consideration.

Here, rather than reading a lengthy portion of Scripture as we do when we read through the Bible in a year, the aim is to ensure that we pause and chew over what God might be saying specifically to us. We abide in Christ for greater fruitfulness (John 15:1–4). We find something we need to respond to. It can lead to confession, intercession or action – sometimes all three.

Through meditation of God's Word we discover where knowing, being and living in Christ interact; the place where we are formed into the person Christ has called us to become.

RELATED SCRIPTURE TO CONSIDER: Psa. 19:7–14; 119: 97–104; Mark 10:35–45; Phil. 4:8–9.

AN ACTION TO TAKE: Take the verses from Psalm 119 above and read them slowly, praying God speaks into your life from the words written there. Stop and reread the words that stand out to you.

A PRAYER TO MAKE: 'Lord, may I take my time in reading Your Word and chew over what it is saying directly to me. Amen.'

Hebrews 4:12–16
'For the word of God is alive and active. Sharper than any double-edged sword, it penetrates even to dividing soul and spirit, joints and marrow; it judges the thoughts and attitudes of the heart.' (v12)

The Bible is unique. Unlike any other book, its words do not create a momentary impact but have the capacity to bring about lasting change within us. It is how God speaks and develops each of us. God's Word, like a seed, takes root within us and germinates, with the potential for producing a fruitful harvest in our lives. The reason we follow Jesus and read God's Word is so we can become fruitful, and, working with others, serve our communities through the church.

It is only by reading God's Word and being convicted by God's Spirit that I have considered and then made major changes to my life, at both the moral and practical level. Once converted, even though I was encouraged not to drink alcohol to excess, I continued to drink heavily with friends every evening. I dismissed the wisdom of others until Scripture revealed that excessive drinking leads to debauchery or, as Ogden Nash, the American poet, said, 'Candy is dandy but liquor is quicker'*.

Scripture acts like yeast. It brings life to all who consume it. Dough remains inert and powerless until yeast initiates the fermentation process. The Word is our staple diet and enables us first to come alive and then grow up into maturity in Christ.

RELATED SCRIPTURE TO CONSIDER: Isa. 55:8–11; Matt. 13:1–23; Acts 2:37–41; Eph. 5:15–20.

AN ACTION TO TAKE: As you open your Bible, invite God's Spirit to enjoy freedom to convict you of those parts of your life which God wants to change.

A PRAYER TO MAKE: 'Lord, please release the yeast of Your Spirit to invigorate the dough that is my mortal life. Amen.'

*Reflections on Ice Breaking (1931)

Hebrews 3:7–19

'So, as the Holy Spirit says: "Today, if you hear his voice, do not harden your hearts as you did in the rebellion, during the time of testing in the wilderness, where your ancestors tested and tried me, though for forty years they saw what I did."' (vv7–9)

The Spirit divides soul and spirit, as we read yesterday. Simply put, the soul is understood as human reason, consciousness and perception. The spirit is the breath, or life, of God within us. It is the spirit that we are invited to follow, for the spirit will always point us in God's direction. Our soul, however, is inclined to serve our human interests rather than God's plans for us.

Life is a series of challenges that demand we make decisions. We can call on past experience, human reason and common sense, all of which are useful aspects of our being. However, once we have yielded to the reality that we are subject to an all-seeing, all-knowing and everywhere-present God, it is His directions we are encouraged to follow.

Leaving Oxford University, with an invitation to join a leading city accountancy firm, with an astute mentor to help develop my career, I chose to join a Christian youth organisation instead. One reason my father was furious with me. My only excuse was the call I felt from God through Scripture, which I could not avoid. That scripture remains critical to my understanding of my life calling, and much of it has been realised through my life to date. Responding to God's Spirit revealed through God's Word may demand we have to make difficult choices.

RELATED SCRIPTURE TO CONSIDER: 2 Sam. 23:1–7; Psa. 95; John 5:36–47; 1 Pet. 1:13–25.

AN ACTION TO TAKE: When God highlights something in the Bible, pause and pray. Ask God, 'How shall I respond?' We are to be led by the Spirit in all things.

A PRAYER TO MAKE: 'Lord, help me to discern between my perspective and Your invitation. Amen.'

Deuteronomy 8

'Be careful to follow every command I am giving you today, so that you may live and increase and may enter and possess the land that the LORD promised on oath to your ancestors.' (v1)

Scripture presents questions. Widely, and critically, analysed throughout history, today few place complete confidence in rationality's ability to answer and resolve them all. Scripture's authority is queried. In an age when fewer people read, many Christians learn more on social media and – from pulpit explanations than from reading the Bible themselves.

Many Christians fail to recognise a scriptural reference unless it comes tagged with chapter and verse. Scripture as a framework for cultural understanding is fast disappearing. There is a danger that we return to a situation Israel experienced in the time of the Judges, when everyone did what was right in their own eyes (eg Judg. 17:6). Israel lacked a king, but we have a King Jesus, who is the Word of God.

There is a valuable tradition formed over time as to how the Church understands Scripture. We may helpfully reflect on this and must take care before departing from the wisdom of those who have gone before us. Indeed, the Bible will always draw us back to Jesus and His foundational command to love God and neighbour (Mark 12:30–31).

So always handle Scripture with respect and take great care to heed its instructions, for it is the very lifeblood upon which faithful and practical Christian discipleship is established and built.

RELATED SCRIPTURE TO CONSIDER: Josh. 5:2–9; Judg. 17:1–6; Luke 11:27–28; Rom. 2:5–11.

AN ACTION TO TAKE: Look to Scripture for guidance in every aspect of your life and always test what others say against it.

A PRAYER TO MAKE: 'Lord, teach me how to live in accordance with Your Word. Amen.'

Obey

Deuteronomy 11:26–32

'When you have taken it over [the Promised Land] and are living there, be sure that you obey all the decrees and laws I am setting before you today.' (vv31b–32)

The Gospel Coalition, an American movement committed to renewing Christian faith, reported in 2020 on the 'scandal of biblical illiteracy'.* It revealed only 36% of committed Christians regularly attend church and personally read the Bible every day. A crisis of 'Bible neglect'.

Yet, Scripture is clear, we cannot navigate our own lives, let alone act as Christ's ambassadors, if we don't know God's intentions set out throughout the Bible (Psa. 119:4–5). We not only fail to grow in knowledge of God and God's ways, we also miss an opportunity to meet with God face to face. For Jesus is God's Word.

Over the last week we have briefly touched on the fact that the Bible offers us different ways to engage with its text, and that without such a daily encounter we can easily miss God's course for our life. There is a crisis of confidence throughout society, heightened by the fears created by the global pandemic. As disciples we hold in our hands God's eternal truth. It offers stability, insight and clear guidance in how we are to live to best effect in an unstable world.

Of course, that's a choice each of us must make for ourselves. It is strongly contested by many voices, yet it is also affirmed by the testimony of millions who have entrusted their lives to the Bible as the handbook for learning to make the most of life.

RELATED SCRIPTURE TO CONSIDER: 1 Chron: 16:7–36; Jer. 29:1–14; John 10:1–18; Rom. 1:8–32.

AN ACTION TO TAKE: I encourage you to join me and engage in a three-year study of God's Word with Search the Scriptures to encourage our spiritual formation. Copies are available from **edwj.org/ja21-18jul**

A PRAYER TO MAKE: 'Lord, may I keep Your Word ever before me, day by day. Amen.'

*https://www.thegospelcoalition.org/article/bible-literacy-crisis/ [accessed 21/03/2021]

Psalm 118:1–4
**'Give thanks to the LORD, for he is good;
his love endures forever.'** (v1)

Over the past few weeks, it might seem there are a lot of responsibilities resting upon our shoulders. We are disciples, following Jesus and seeking to do God's will in our world. The great news is that it remains God's will, and we are channels allowing God to reveal His way through our lives.

Having failed my eleven plus exam, I could see my parents' great disappointment. I endeavoured with all my might to work harder at school to please them. But I still didn't do very well. My problem was responding to what I thought they wanted and not to what I knew I could do. Too often we respond to God like this, assuming God demands of us things we can't do. How often do we use the words 'ought' or 'should' to speak of our Christian life; for example, 'I ought to pray more'?

The statement, 'Pray as you can, not as you can't', applies to all of the Christian life. It's only as I let go of seeking to perform for others and serve my own inner compass, that I found rest. God invites us to find comfort and calm in the truth that we are loved immeasurably, regardless of what others may demand or say about our performance.

The encouragement to Christian service rises as we discover more of God's enduring love and find that living the Christian life is something we want to do, not something we feel we should do.

RELATED SCRIPTURE TO CONSIDER: Psa 4:6–8; 127; Mark 6:30–34; Matt. 11:25–30.

AN ACTION TO TAKE: Take time to understand what it is you are striving for, and ask yourself whether this is what God truly wants you to live for?

A PRAYER TO MAKE: 'Lord, thank You that Your love endures forever, and that I am forever invited to rest within Your arms. Amen.'

Looking for summer reading? We've got it covered...

Now is the perfect time to explore these books...

Specks and Planks: Stories of Hope, Humility and Humanity

Jeff Lucas

Staying in the Boat: And Other Things I Wish I'd Known

Jeff Lucas

The Dog Who Thought His Name Was No

Judy Moore

Unwavering: The Power of Choice (An Inspiring Women Book)

Jen Baker

Unshakeable Confidence
(An Inspiring Women Book)

Jen Baker

Life Together: The Family Devotional

Steve and Bekah Legg

Cold Cups of Tea and Hiding in the Loo:
An Honest Look at Parenting

Annie Wilmot

The Activity Bible (Ages 4–7)

The Activity Bible (Ages 7–11)

**To order these titles and dive into your next great read, visit
waverleyabbeyresources.org**

Psalm 118:5–14

'It is better to take refuge in the LORD than to trust in humans. It is better to take refuge in the LORD than to trust in princes.' (vv8–9)

It's difficult separating news from views. Every piece of personal news analysis carries within it 'unrealised persuaders'. These are the result of our culture, upbringing and inherent prejudices, amongst other factors. What appears objective has already been through our inbuilt bias filters.

Growing up, I was taught always to trust a policeman! Now we hear an increasing number of troubling stories that challenge this advice. Even that statement will provoke a reaction based upon our 'hidden persuaders'. As Jesus' disciples we must first decide if we're able to place complete confidence in God, and then consider if we can see fellow humans as image bearers of our God.

Scripture clearly tells us that the human heart is desperately wicked (Jer. 17:9) but we are told by God to view everyone as made in God's image and so everyone is invited to find salvation and redemption in Him. Remember the thief crucified alongside Jesus (Luke 23:39–43)?

God was prepared to offer me a refuge, and whatever my critics know, I will always know far more about my darker side than they can ever fathom. God also knows what I know, and more, yet chooses to forgive and love me – you too if you turn to God. Surrendering my preconceptions and choosing to live by God's Word will prove challenging on a daily basis.

RELATED SCRIPTURE TO CONSIDER: Prov. 4:20–27; Jer. 17:7–10; John 2:23–25; Rev 3:14–22.

AN ACTION TO TAKE: Are there obstacles that prevent you from taking refuge in God and embracing God's Word as completely reliable?

A PRAYER TO MAKE: 'Lord, guide me through the many news stories I'm bombarded with and help me to view them through the truth of Your Word. Amen.'

Write to **micha@edwj.org** and I'll write back personally and in confidence as soon as I can.

Psalm 118:15–24

'I will not die but live, and will proclaim what the LORD has done. The LORD has chastened me severely, but he has not given me over to death.' (vv17–18)

Recently, on a retreat looking at God and chronic illness (a long-term condition for which there is no cure), I discovered people's tremendous courage and God's inexhaustible grace. Everyone involved experienced continuous pain, and practical restrictions to living and working as they would like. Yet, each spoke of the life that God brought to them in very difficult human circumstances.

It's easy to use a word like 'resilience' (the ability to endure and overcome a significant experience), but altogether different when talking with those who require resilience on a daily, even hourly basis. Finding God within what many might see as impossible situations is both a testimony to that person's qualities and an aspect of wonder at the nature of God's compassionate message of love. It's one thing to praise God if healed of my pain, as the lame man did at the gate Beautiful (Acts 3:8); altogether something else to remain faith filled in the face of continuous illness (Job 13:15).

I have nothing but respect and gratitude to those who persevere in faith, though they do not enjoy the life they might want. Their testimony offers confidence for us all that God's Word is true. Such testimony silences my complaint and invites me to choose to entrust myself once more to God's promise.

RELATED SCRIPTURE TO CONSIDER: Josh. 24:14–21; Prov. 3:5–8; Acts 3:1–10; Rev. 1:9–18.

AN ACTION TO TAKE: *Bouncing Forwards* is a book by Patrick Regan that addresses the issue of resilience: pick up your copy from **edwj.org/ja21-21jul**

A PRAYER TO MAKE: 'Lord, I choose to place my hope in You, even when I am confused and uncertain. Give me courage when I find myself in the dark. Amen.'

John 13:1–17

'Now that I, your LORD and Teacher, have washed your feet, you also should wash one another's feet.' (v14)

Elephants travel in groups, their pace set by that of the slowest. This is a principle we might embrace as God's Church. Perhaps it's the equivalent of the US marines slogan, 'Leave no one behind'. As disciples we have a responsibility to ensure we are vigilant in caring for our own.

If Jesus washed His disciples' feet, then encouraged us to do the same, what might that mean for God's Church today? Perhaps that we demonstrate in practice this deep commitment to care for each other.

In their 2011 survey, the Campaign to End Loneliness discovered that 45% of people felt lonely, 'some of the time'. The loneliest are found amongst those aged under twenty-five and over sixty-five.* As the Church, we enjoy a hospitable space, hopefully open to all. Indeed, Archbishop William Temple described the Church as the only group that exists for the benefit of its non-members.** Still, we can start by offering friendship and welcome to those within the Church. This will prove very attractive to many throughout our communities who suffer from loneliness.

Jesus said that it was the quality of the love exhibited by His followers that would make sense of the gospel to the stranger. Let's create loving hubs of hospitality everywhere, available to everyone.

RELATED SCRIPTURE TO CONSIDER: Deut. 10:12–22; Job 29:7–17; Luke 5:17–26; John 13:31–35.

AN ACTION TO TAKE: Some of us find forming relationships easier than others. But let's each commit to encouraging at least one person every day.

A PRAYER TO MAKE: 'Lord, I choose to place my hope in You, even when I am confused and uncertain. Give me courage when I find myself in the dark. Amen.'

*https://www.campaigntoendloneliness.org/loneliness-research/[accessed 21/03/2021]
**Recalled as a personal dictum in 'Letter from the Archbishop of the West Indies' in *Theology* (1956), vol. 59. *Oxford Essential Quotations* (4th ed.) edited by Susan Ratcliffe (Oxford: OUP, 2016) [accessed 21/03/2021]

1 Thessalonians 5:11–15
**'Therefore encourage one another and build each
other up, just as in fact you are doing.'** (v11)

Clive Calver once wrote a book entitled, *With a Church Like This,
Who Needs Satan?* A hard hitting, perhaps slightly unfair title, but
one that captures the shock many of us feel when discovering
how much criticism there is within the Church. This is not just aimed
at those who might practise the historic Christian faith with some
differences to our own preference, but also refers to the criticism
existing between members of the same church.

Jesus calls us to love, not criticise, one another. When I'm criticised,
I react and often hit back verbally. However, if I am encouraged I
am more likely to flourish and become more receptive to legitimate
concerns about both character and behaviour.

That's because encouragement builds our confidence. Barnabas
comes alongside the outcast Saul, now renamed Paul, and
encourages him. Consequently, one of the greatest witnesses to the
Christian faith is enabled to realise his ministry.

I fear, looking back from eternity, we shall see many people who
only realised a portion of their potential because they were subdued
through the criticism of others where they might have flourished
under encouragement. Jesus was a great encourager, as his post-
resurrection breakfast with Peter revealed.

RELATED SCRIPTURE TO CONSIDER: Psa. 23; John 21:15–23; Acts 4:32–37; 11:19–30.

AN ACTION TO TAKE: Encouragement is so much easier today. We can drop a
text to someone, post a message on their social media presence or invite
them out for a coffee. Set yourself a goal to encourage two people every
week.

A PRAYER TO MAKE: 'Lord, may I both receive encouragement and become a
source of encouragement to others. Amen.'

Isaiah 40:25–31

'He gives strength to the weary and increases the power of the weak. Even youths grow tired and weary, and young men stumble and fall; but those who hope in the LORD will renew their strength.' (vv29–31a)

As we age, things slow down. Things such as our healing processes. When I cut myself preparing food, my finger takes so much longer repairing itself. We also face a decline in strength, mobility and energy levels. Within, however, I confess to feeling a lot more like Caleb. I retain enthusiasm for fresh challenges. True, I don't always calculate the odds of my achieving such ideas born of enthusiasm, but gradually God has taught me two things.

First, I'm to direct my energy in the most productive way possible. So, having known a call to prayer which I have taken years to respond to with both enthusiasm and effort I now am highly committed to a daily prayer rhythm that suits me. I have also recognised that I shall enjoy ever larger amounts of time to pray as my body makes its way towards its inevitable departure from this earth.

Second, when I do what God is calling me to, I feel a fresh vitality throughout my whole being. It's as if serving God's purpose rejuvenates me. I really do feel as if I might fly. Serving God is what we are born for.

It is encouraging to know that as we listen and respond to God, there is never a time when we find ourselves eliminated from God's purpose. Ours is a productive life once we accept that we live under God's instruction and that, even as we serve God, we become more of who God created us to be.

RELATED SCRIPTURE TO CONSIDER: Num. 13:21–33; 14:24–25; Josh. 14:6–15; 1 Cor. 4:7–18.

AN ACTION TO TAKE: Consider if you want to continue in God's active service right up until departure for eternity. If so, ask God to continue to use you, renew you and deploy you on active service.

A PRAYER TO MAKE: 'Lord, help me to live each day serving Your purposes whilst renewed by Your strength. Amen.'

Run

Hebrews 12:1–4

'Therefore, since we are surrounded by such a great cloud of witnesses, let us throw off everything that hinders and the sin that so easily entangles.' (v1a)

This past week we have taken a look at various challenges Scripture presents us with. There are different ways we can engage with God's Word. Rich and varied ways in which we are able to encounter Jesus. Yet, through God's invitation the Bible invites us to discover how it is we can learn to love, live for and serve God in every aspect of our life experience.

This is a book relevant to every age and in all circumstances. It presents us with God's challenge to live our life in full and faithful service to a purpose that was sown within us from before the moment of our conception (Jer. 1:5).

One thing I like to reflect on is that the Bible contains the testimonies of a number of that ever-increasing cloud of witnesses that surround us. I think it is probably my age that focuses me with excitement on joining such witnesses. We have the remarkable stories of mortals like ourselves, who wrestled with all the same challenges as we do and yet found God's way. By surrendering and serving God they navigated often difficult paths through life and entered into their eternal rest. I look forward to my future departure whilst leaving a testimony of a faithful witness for my family, at least, to draw encouragement from.

RELATED SCRIPTURE TO CONSIDER: Deut. 31:1–8; 1 Sam. 17:45–51; Psa. 119:169–176; Rev 1:1–8.

AN ACTION TO TAKE: Consider which character in the Bible inspires you, and why?

A PRAYER TO MAKE: 'Lord, help me to walk faithfully throughout my life, serving You with courage and conviction until I see You face to face. Amen.'

Jeremiah 31:30–34
**'Instead, everyone will die for their own sin; whoever eats
sour grapes their own teeth will be set on edge.'** (v30)

An American friend always tells me that as well as the Statue of
Liberty in New York's harbour, a Statue of Responsibility must
be built in San Francisco Bay. He feels we cannot enjoy liberty
without responsibility.

There's some truth in this. We cannot enjoy freedom without
the exercise of restraint. In most cases, we rely on common sense,
backed up by legal enforcement; for example, if I insist on breaking
and entering to steal and invade someone's privacy.

God generously extends freedom of choice to every one of us. He
also sets out how we might enjoy fullness of life. Placed within our
hands is the possibility for setting our own course. As with every
choice there are consequences, both seen and unseen. Choices
that later prove to have been bad present us with the opportunity for
another chance to choose, yet leave us to deal with the consequences
of that bad decision.

Hopefully, we learn how to make good choices from the bad ones
we are bound to make. This is part of our learning process. The place
to start in considering any choice is to review what God says in His
Word. We can also find people we trust who equally love and serve
Jesus. Common wisdom advocates that two heads are better than
one, something taken straight from the Bible (Eccl. 4:9–12).

RELATED SCRIPTURE TO CONSIDER: Deut. 30:19–20; 2 Sam. 12:1–25; Eccl. 4:9–12;
Acts 15:22–35.

AN ACTION TO TAKE: Are there decisions you regret? Bring them before God and
ask for His forgiveness and help in making fresh decisions going forward.
You may need the encouragement and support of Christian friends.

A PRAYER TO MAKE: 'Lord, guide me in my decision making every day. Amen.'

Psalm 51:1–9
**'Have mercy on me, O God, according to your unfailing love;
according to your great compassion blot out my transgressions.
Wash away all my iniquity and cleanse me from my sin.'** (vv1–2)

On recognising I've made a bad decision, my first port of call is confession. Sadly, like Adam, when confronted I rise up in self-defence and look to point the finger. Adam pointed one at Eve and the other at God: 'The *woman you* put here with me' (Gen. 3:12, emphasis added). Our need to justify ourselves is strong, yet who can justify themselves before God? No one.

Once we recognise a bad decision, the first thing we must do is acknowledge it. Our instinct is often to consider how we can either disguise it or lay it at someone else's door. This is deceitful, the currency of Satan.

It takes courage to own our mistakes, yet everyone makes mistakes. Eve shows us the best way to respond (Gen. 3:13). Sometimes we are aware of the harm such decisions will cause, and here we must consider if we can make any restitution for the actual damage done. It may cost us something, yet it cost Jesus everything to reverse the curse of Adam's poor decision making.

God, of course, already knows, so any excuses we make are merely an attempt to save face. And this only ever for a human audience. God sees all and we are known for truly who we are. It may prove painful, but our ultimate purpose is to live at peace with God rather than serve some personal profile of our own imagining.

RELATED SCRIPTURE TO CONSIDER: Gen. 3:1–13; Prov. 28:9–13; Jam. 4:7–12; 1 John 1:5–10.

AN ACTION TO TAKE: Take time each evening to review your day and consider if there are things to confess to God.

A PRAYER TO MAKE: 'Lord, forgive my sins (name any that come to mind) and cleanse and restore me. Amen.'

I Am My Lord's

Psalm 51:10–12

'Create in me a pure heart, O God, and renew a steadfast spirit within me. Do not cast me from your presence or take your Holy Spirit from me.' (vv10–11)

The purpose of confessing to God is so that we can be cleansed, and then to nurture and nourish the new heart God promises to all who turn to Jesus. In an instant age, when I assume that my request is fulfilled immediately, it's easy to assume that our friendship with God is a transactional one.

A transaction is the simple purchase of something. However, I cannot purchase, nor indeed earn, forgiveness from God. There is only one eternally significant transaction, and that was completed by Jesus. As Charles Wesley wrote, 'Tis done, the great transaction's done, I am my Lord's, and he is mine; He drew me, and I followed on, Charmed to confess the voice divine.'

No one can add or subtract from God's redemptive work. However, as God draws me and I choose to follow Him, my life becomes more of a spiritual building site. Ground must be cleared and foundations sunk before any structure can begin to emerge. Salvation may be secured in a moment; spiritual formation the work of a lifetime.

So I daily return to God's Word, I make confession and I invest in co-operating with God in allowing a pure heart to be crafted within me. Only God is pure; but God promises He will clean me up and also raise me up to who I was created to be.

RELATED SCRIPTURE TO CONSIDER: Prov. 3:1–12; John 20:24–29; Rom 10:8–15.

AN ACTION TO TAKE: Consider training in spiritual formation and growing your own personal life of faith with Waverley Abbey College **edwj.org/ja21-28jul**

A PRAYER TO MAKE: 'Lord, as I confess my sins, I invite You to help me to grow up into maturity in Christ. Amen.'

'From the hymn, *O Happy Day*, https://www.youtube.com/watch?v=043We8Rc90U [accessed 21/03/2021]

Psalm 51:13–17
**'Then I will teach transgressors your ways, so
that sinners will turn back to you.'** (v13)

When I travelled the world on missions many years ago, it was
essential to pay attention to what I drank. On one trip to Nigeria,
I drank some contaminated water and was sicker than I have
ever been. I needed some medication which cleansed my system and
restored my health.

This is what confession achieves. It washes my system, dislodges
the fall out from sin and equips me in four vital ways.

First, I am empowered to reveal and communicate the ways of God
in terms others can understand. I am thrilled that I have received
feedback from those who don't describe themselves as Christians
but are finding *Every Day With Jesus* a source of challenge and
encouragement.

Next, I know that I'm forgiven and accepted by God. The shadow of
my shame is dispersed by the light of God's grace. Whenever I stumble
into the shadows again, I confess and step into the sun's warmth.

Third, I discover a strong desire to worship God, declaring my love
and confidence in the unseen yet ever-present Lord and Master of my
life: worship is one element of the Church's prayer language.

Finally, I am humbled in recognition that God loves me, warts and all.
I can do nothing to enable God to love me more. I can simply respond
to a boundless acceptance and recognise that this is never about me,
or us, but entirely and always about God.

RELATED SCRIPTURE TO CONSIDER: Psa. 103:7–19; Isa. 1:15–20; 1 Tim. 1:12–19;
1 John 1.

AN ACTION TO TAKE: Look back over today's reading and consider how you might
establish this four-part rhythm in your daily routine. It is the foundation for
mine.

A PRAYER TO MAKE: 'Lord, help to humble myself so that I can step from the
shadows of my life into the warmth of Your embrace, every day. Amen.'

Hebrews 5:5–10

'Son though he was, he learned obedience from what he suffered and, once made perfect, he became the source of eternal salvation for all who obey him' (vv8–9)

Suffering is not something we want eagerly to embrace. We observe Jesus' life and the great suffering He endured in fulfilling God's salvation purpose. Yet, Scripture doesn't avoid the issue of suffering. It is quite a challenge to accept the idea that Jesus' suffering was part of God's redemptive process.

Scripture encourages us that, whatever suffering we experience, Christ knows of it in intimate detail for He too suffered. Peter in his epistles encouraged faithfulness in the face of suffering, which the Christian must anticipate as one element of our mortal experience.

This is one reason that Waverley Abbey Trust actively encourages, and makes resources available to, the suffering church. Scripture's clear and states, 'Carry each other's burdens, and in this way you will fulfil the law of Christ' (Gal. 6:2).

I am always moved by the faithfulness of those who suffer. The nature of the suffering can be because of their faith and I had the privilege of serving the persecuted church for 12 years or because they're navigating chronic illness or some other malady. The fact that Jesus is present in the worst of human experience is, for me, a tremendous statement on the depth of God's love. The question always remains; are we able to find God when life is painful?

RELATED SCRIPTURE TO CONSIDER: Isa. 43:1–13; 2 Cor. 4:16–18; 1 Pet. 4; Heb. 4:14–16.

AN ACTION TO TAKE: If you suffer, are you able to find Jesus in your struggles? If so, how? Also, let's pray and practically find ways to bear the burdens of others. Donations to *Every Day With Jesus* go to ensure these notes are available in different languages to the suffering church. You can donate here: **edwj.org/ja21-30jul**

A PRAYER TO MAKE: 'Lord, encourage me in my suffering and help me to become an encourager of others through my prayers and actions. Amen.'

WAVERLEY ABBEY TRUST

COLLEGE   RESOURCES   HOUSE

waverleyabbeycollege.ac.uk   waverleyabbeyresources.org   waverleyabbeyhouse.org

Waverley Abbey Trust

We are a charity serving Christians around the world with practical resources and teaching. We support you to grow in your Christian faith, understand the times in which we live, and serve God in every sphere of life.

The three main areas we focus on are:

- **Mental Health and Wellbeing**
- **Leadership**
- **Spiritual Formation**

waverleyabbey.org

John 12:20–33

'Very truly I tell you, unless a grain of wheat falls to the ground and dies, it remains only a single seed. But if it dies, it produces many seeds.' (v24)

One thing that takes time to adjust to is the fact that, as disciples, we surrender all rights to our life to Jesus. However, we struggle because what Scripture calls 'the flesh' fights back. Our natural human inclination is to resist God (Rom. 8:5–8). We live in a constant struggle between surrender and self-expression. Indeed, life is a journey in which, like John the Baptist, we wrestle with our need to shrink in stature and visibility so that Jesus might grow and become clearly visible in us and our lives (John 3:30).

Jesus directs our attention to the rhythm of nature. Any gardener knows when planting a seed that it needs the appropriate conditions to germinate and produce the promised harvest displayed colourfully on its packet. Germination is to emerge from dormancy and come into existence and grow. It's the perfect picture of spiritual formation. Slowly we grow to become more like Jesus. As seeds we must die to self if we are to produce a harvest under God's guidance and to God's glory (Gal. 2:20–21).

No surprises here. We start as a babe in Christ, with our objective to become perfect as our heavenly Father is perfect (Matt. 5:48). This demands attention to what naturally stirs within us and serves as the basis on which we instinctively take decisions. The path of discipleship is one of consistent vigilance as we learn and practise our faith. We must be intentional if we want to go further with Jesus every day.

RELATED SCRIPTURE TO CONSIDER: Psa. 40:1–5; Prov. 22:1–12; Eph. 4:17–32; 5:1–20.

AN ACTION TO TAKE: What barriers to the full surrender of your life to Jesus come to mind? Are there steps you might take to break such barriers down?

A PRAYER TO MAKE: 'Lord, help me to co-operate with Your Holy Spirit in decreasing, so Jesus might shine more brightly. Amen.'

Ephesians 4:11–16
**'until we all reach unity in the faith and in the knowledge
of the Son of God and become mature, attaining to the
whole measure of the fullness of Christ.'** (v13)

Spiritual formation is a journey, and never a destination. There are certain points where we pause and reflect to consider where we have come from. But very soon the Spirit summons us to get up and go to an as yet unseen land (Gen. 12:1). We build our confidence in God's future from the experience we have developed in journeying with God. It's why it is good to pause, reflect and pray in God's Word daily.

The challenge for every Christian is that we are in a state of perpetual becoming, right up until we cross the threshold death presents and into God's arms. I've no knowledge of how I shall stand before God on that day. However, Scripture encourages each of us to determine how fervently we invest our energy into growing up into the fullness of God, in preparation.

Our Christian progress lies within our own choices. We will face both barriers and reversals. However, character is forged through perseverance and finding the fullness of God in every eventuality. Each challenge offers an opportunity for us to press deeper into the truth who is God, or falter in our commitment.

Even if we falter, this is simply an opportunity to reconsider what we truly seek from life and how we will therefore choose to live. Spiritual formation is indeed a path that frequently winds back on itself, whilst making progress towards Christian maturity.

RELATED SCRIPTURE TO CONSIDER: Lam. 3:19–40; Isa. 46:3–13; Phil. 1:3–11; Heb. 10:19–25.

AN ACTION TO TAKE: How do you cope when you appear to be back peddling on your discipleship path?

A PRAYER TO MAKE: 'Lord, may I keep my eyes on the prize and press on each and every day in pursuit of God's fullness. Amen.'

1 Samuel 7:3–9

'So Samuel said to all the Israelites, "If you are returning to the LORD with all your hearts, then rid yourselves of the foreign gods and the Ashtoreths and commit yourselves to the LORD and serve him only, and he will deliver you out of the hand of the Philistines."' (v3)

Some say, 'the road to hell is paved with good intentions'. The first person recorded as saying this was Bernard of Clairvaux, the leading Cistercian of the twelfth century. He declared, '*l'enfer est plein de bonnes volontés et désirs*' or 'hell is full of good wishes and desires'. Waverley Abbey, near Farnham in Surrey, where I write *EDWJ*, was the first Cistercian monastery in England and I ruminate on his words every time I pray walking around its ruins.

An intention is something planned, yet is never more than an idea until put into practice. Many of us have made authentic responses to God, only to admit some time later that they amounted to little by way of practical effect. One good reason why Jesus talks of the importance of fruit as evidence of a life surrendered to God.

We have discovered the importance and power of confession and restoration. Whilst this remains an inexhaustible process, if we keep doing the same thing time after time expecting different results, some would define this as madness.

Permanent change involves a complete adjustment in behaviour. Once forgiven, it might be useful both to ask God to show me why it is that I seem to make the same mistakes continually, and to create some different slabs with which to pave my pilgrim's path; a pilgrim being anyone on a journey in pursuit of God.

RELATED SCRIPTURE TO CONSIDER: Num. 23:18–20; Psa. 18:1–6; Matt. 7:15–23; 18:21–35.

AN ACTION TO TAKE: What's the harvest you see in your life today? What changes in behaviour would it be good to consider?

A PRAYER TO MAKE: 'Lord, help me in making those adjustments that enable me to live a more fruitful life serving You. Amen.'

1 Samuel 7:10–12

'Then Samuel took a stone and set it up between Mizpah and Shen. He named it Ebenezer, saying, "Thus far the LORD has helped us."' (v12)

When growing up I noted that some houses had names, and amongst these was 'Ebenezer'. An unusual name for a house, I thought, until I discovered its true meaning. It is a word we should each declare at the start of our day, acknowledging that God has sustained us to this point.

As we read these scriptures we are presented with the truth that 'the battle is the LORD's' (2 Chron. 20:15). One of my challenges is to avoid seeking to organise tomorrow before it arrives. Not so much the practicalities of daily living, but the anxieties I have over larger matters. It's as if I want to see outcomes ahead of time, so I can make the best decisions possible. But we are not able to see the future.

We do, however, worship a God in whose hands the future, including my own, can be safely entrusted. As Samuel honoured God, He took care of Israel's enemies (v10).

One final thought: Ebenezer simply translated means 'stone of help'. It was Peter's faith that Jesus declared as the rock upon which the Church would be built, whilst He provides its cornerstone. And we, the global Church, are the new Israel. As the Church, let's review our calling to live as God's ambassadors for a world in need, daily reminding ourselves, and each other, 'Thus far the LORD has helped us'.

RELATED SCRIPTURE TO CONSIDER: 2 Chron. 20:1–24; 1 Sam. 17:41–47; Matt. 16:13–20; Eph. 2:19–22.

AN ACTION TO TAKE: Take some time to identify and consider your anxieties about your tomorrows yet to come. Can you find God in them and find your rest in God? Maybe set up a stone outside your front door, a reminder every time you leave your house.

A PRAYER TO MAKE: 'Lord, thank You that thus far You have helped me. May I find my confidence in You for my tomorrows yet to be. Amen.'

Children

1 Samuel 8:1–5

'But his sons did not follow his ways. They turned aside after dishonest gain and accepted bribes and perverted justice.' (v3)

For many parents their greatest concern is their children's future. Be it education, the friends they hang out with or their spiritual development, the level of angst they can create is high. If the future is in God's hands, our children's future presents a significant worry.

One problem is the fear many have of the way they might be judged within their church community. I served as a church leader for 18 years and can honestly say parents are not responsible for the decisions their children take. It is so very hard as a parent to release someone you have poured your love into for 18 years into a world you never feel they are adequately prepared to navigate.

On reflection, I was once that 18-year-old. I confidently left home without a backward glance. I made it, albeit with many mistakes I'd avoid if I had my time over again.

The second anxiety is our desire to see our children safe and secure in a faith-filled friendship with God. Sadly, here we can only act as a positive influence. The practical disciplines of prayer, Bible reading and service which our children observe in our own lives offer the best advertisement for the benefits of the Christian life. These are the creative ways we try to make sense of our faith to them as they grow up, together with the ongoing prayers of our loving, often wounded hearts. Always remember, God loves prodigals!

RELATED SCRIPTURE TO CONSIDER: Prov. 1:8–19; Mal. 4; Luke 15:11–32; Eph. 6:1–4.

AN ACTION TO TAKE: Find a way to ask your children about their faith journey – out of interest and not to check up on them.

A PRAYER TO MAKE: 'Lord, may the seeds of faith planted in the lives of our children germinate and produce a harvest. Amen.'

Consequences

1 Samuel 8:19–22
**'But the people refused to listen to Samuel. "No!"
they said. "We want a king over us."'** (v19)

The guidance, 'Be careful what you ask for', has a long history. It comes from Aesop's fables created around 260 BC.

Samuel served as Israel's last judge, and the first prophet after Moses. Despite his wise counsel, the people believed they knew better. They set aside his advice to pursue their desire for a king to rule over them. Samuel, initially irritated, takes his frustration to God, who guides his response. Taking our concerns to God ahead of expressing them publicly is a good principle to follow.

Wisdom teaches that choices made from direct comparison with others misdirects us. The superficial good will conceal many compromises and challenges beneath. Samuel knows of the surrender of personal freedoms appointing a king will require. The people just clamoured for robust leadership, ready to surrender personal responsibility that they didn't appreciate.

Samuel, having expressed his preference to God, seeks to serve the best interests of the Israelites. God asks Samuel to let go and let God. What was to Samuel a bad decision, was in fact God's choice. Samuel knew not to stand in God's way.

It was Abraham Lincoln who said, 'Most folks are about as happy as they make up their minds to be'.* Let's learn to take responsibility for where we find ourselves and seek God there. We might find God knows more than we thought He did.

RELATED SCRIPTURE TO CONSIDER: Psa. 37:1–9; Prov. 13:3–20; Matt. 7:7–12; James 4:1–10.

AN ACTION TO TAKE: Establish the discipline of taking time to consult with God before taking action; and trust God's advice, like Samuel did.

A PRAYER TO MAKE: 'Lord, help me to learn to pause and pray before reacting and responding to opportunity and challenge. Amen.'

*Attributed to Lincoln by Dr. Frank Crane about 50 years after his death, https://quoteinvestigator.com/2012/10/20/happy-minds/ [accessed 21/03/2021]

Luke 21:34–38
'Be always on the watch, and pray that you may be able to escape all that is about to happen, and that you may be able to stand before the Son of Man.' (v36)

A priority is what's most important to us. In our busy lives, we soon discover there are any number actively competing against each other. Life quickly becomes a struggle for survival. We lose perspective and then lose peace of mind.

Jesus' priority was to do the will of His Father in heaven (John 6:38). It follows that, as a disciple, this is also my priority. But how do I accomplish this in a world where time's at a premium?

Our problem lies in our attempt to separate God from our everyday reality. Jesus was fully integrated into the life of His time and culture. He spent 30 years, in which we imagine He lived like His peers, before being called into ministry by the Holy Spirit. Even then, He continued to engage in everyday life on the road.

God is always our priority in the busyness of life. I have responsibilities that demand my time, yet I can deal with them always focused on God. I may lose sight of Him momentarily, yet I have built touchpoints throughout my day reminding me I'm about my Father's business.

These touchpoints are my navigation system. They ensure I return to my true course when distracted by external events or my own unruly emotions. For example, I set my alarm for noon and pause to pray the Lord's Prayer, amongst others, as a moment to take stock and ensure I remain on course.

RELATED SCRIPTURE TO CONSIDER: Job 11:13–19; Psa. 32:6–11; Matt. 7:21–23; John 6:32–40.

AN ACTION TO TAKE: Create some touchpoints in your day and consider joining one of our courses that explore making sense of God in everyday life: **waverleyabbeyresources.org**.

A PRAYER TO MAKE: 'Lord, help to remember that I am here to do the will of God, which I can discover in all of my responsibilities. Amen.'

Luke 21:8–19
**'But make up your mind not to worry beforehand
how you will defend yourselves.'** (v14)

Besieged by 24/7 news and views, being selective is difficult. There's a thin line between balanced information and feeling overwhelmed. We need some news to fuel our prayers, yet too much and we risk elevated stress levels, disturbed sleep patterns and increased anxiety.

Jesus says that life happens around us and that we're not to worry. We may ourselves be impacted by the worrying news stories, such as on those still recovering from long Covid, yet we have in Jesus sufficient resources to manage how this affects our state of mind.

Whilst agencies responsibly scramble to devise approaches and solutions to the impact life exerts on all of us, the Bible dares to suggest that all we need to confound those forces that besiege us, both real and imagined, is God's Word.

Standing firm, for me, is a decision of the will. There are rhythms I have developed that help me manage the impact of worry, both in the present and about the future. My morning prayer and silent contemplation are permanent fixtures. My refusal to engage with news apart from headlines on my phone, and never after 6.00pm, is my choice in helping manage my news diet.

This remains a huge subject, but again boils down to the nature of my encounter with God, directly and in fellowship with others, and consequently how I structure my daily life.

RELATED SCRIPTURE TO CONSIDER: Psa. 23; Prov. 10:11–32; 1 Cor. 15:42–58; 1 Pet. 5:6–10.

AN ACTION TO TAKE: Ask yourself the degree and the ways in which 24/7 news impacts your life. How does this influence your perspective upon God's Word and God's promise?

A PRAYER TO MAKE: 'Lord, in times of difficulty may I first acknowledge my concerns and then look to Your Word for encouragement. Amen.'

Where Is God?

Psalm 10:1–7
**'He says to himself, "Nothing will ever shake me."
He swears, "No one will ever do me harm."'** (v6)

When life is tough, we often complain at the apparent ease of another's life experience. Such comparisons are based on our assumptions about the life we're observing. But we only see the outward appearance. Jesus makes it clear that it is the heart within that counts. For what comes from the heart poisons the whole person (Matt. 12:34). We can never know the realities that lie beneath the skin. Humility requires us to think only the best of another (Rom. 12:3).

Such comparisons produce resentment, or our indignation at having been treated badly. Of course, what is really under scrutiny is our own assumptions about what we deserve from life. When tragedy strikes we need to find some solid ground on which to stand. This is in short supply, and we assume we can create it by criticising others. In pain we strike out to protect ourselves, unlike Jesus' example.

God seems distant and we see others succeeding who we feel don't deserve their apparent success. Now it's best to call out to God, who hears the prayers of the lowly and wounded (Psa. 10:17–18). If we learn to appeal to God immediately when disappointed, disillusioned or despondent, then we can save ourselves from rubbing salt into the wound. Salt may help the healing process, but is a healing born of self-induced pain.

RELATED SCRIPTURE TO CONSIDER: Psa. 22; Isa. 53:7–9; Matt. 15:10–20; Luke 6:43–49.

AN ACTION TO TAKE: Take responsibility for yourself and look to God. Don't criticise others. What are the implications for living like this for your daily life?

A PRAYER TO MAKE: 'Lord, You alone are consistent and from You alone might I receive life in all its fullness. Amen' (see John 10:10).

1 Chronicles 16:1–6
'He [David] appointed some of the Levites to minister before the ark of the LORD, to extol, thank, and praise the LORD, the God of Israel:' (v4)

Worship has grown to be central in church life. Generally regarded as singing today, worship is in fact to declare God's renown; the recognition of God's achievements, and our admiration, respect and commitment to God. We worship God in many ways – from our prayer and Bible reading to the way we choose to live our life.

However, singing has always played its part. No matter the quality of our voice, we are all instructed to make a joyful sound for the Lord (Psa. 100:2). Song, increasingly rare within social gatherings, does feature on special occasions such as birthdays. We honour someone by name with a well-known anthem.

In the fourth century, Athanasius, one of the church fathers, encouraged singing, in particular the psalms, not because they *ex*-press our love for God, but rather *im*-press God's love upon our heart.* In other words, we are actually drawing God's love into our lives rather than simply declaring our love towards God.

Worship always reinforces what we know to be true of God within us. It is central to our spiritual formation. It's one reason I often read Scripture aloud even when alone – I'm drinking from God's well whilst also announcing God's reality. In my morning prayers, whilst I cannot really carry a tune, I do chant the psalms aloud. Christianity is indeed poetry in motion.

RELATED SCRIPTURE TO CONSIDER: Psa.63:1–8; Job 1:20–22; Luke 1:46–55; 67–79.

AN ACTION TO TAKE: Consider singing some of your favourite, Scripture-based songs aloud every day. And why not consider chanting a psalm a day?

A PRAYER TO MAKE: 'Lord, I sing praise to You for You are my fortress and my God on whom I can rely. Amen' (see Psa. 59:17).

*Athanasius, *A Letter to Marcellinus*

1 Chronicles 16:8–14
'Sing to him, sing praise to him; tell of all his wonderful acts.' (v9)

The challenge in all worship, from singing to living, is to stay focused on God, not on ourselves. We might describe our hunger for God, or the challenges we face, yet only as part of our ongoing journey with God. Without God I can do nothing (John 15:5).

Waverley Abbey sits on the site of the first Cistercian monastery in Britain. Monastics were laity who chose community life and adopted a rhythm of simplicity, prayer and work. Simplicity meant keeping daily life as clear of distraction as possible. Inspired by the Psalms, they established a structure to pause and pray seven times a day (Psa. 119:164).

These were moments to pause and refocus. Many of these were just a 15-minute pause, like we might break up our working day with a coffee. However, they would sing a hymn, chant a psalm, read a few verses of Scripture and offer up a prayer. A bell was rung, and those close to the chapel would gather there. Others would simply pause in the fields, their work largely farming, and pray where they stood.

It's a simple and well tried structure. It doesn't need community, nor a pattern of seven pauses. It does require some effort. My bell is my phone alarm set to remind me of my rhythm of daily prayer. Lockdown has been a joy, to pause and pray alongside my wife, as together we tell of God's wonderful acts.

RELATED SCRIPTURE TO CONSIDER: Psa. 27; 130:5–8; Mark 6:30–46; John 15:1–17.

AN ACTION TO TAKE: Take a look at the ruins near Farnham, and read the story of those first Cistercians in Britain. Read about Waverley Abbey at **edwj.org/ja21-10aug** Consider visiting, and make sure to let us know you are coming so we can say hello.

A PRAYER TO MAKE: 'Lord, guide me in establishing a pause and worship rhythm for my everyday life. Amen.'

*Application*

# WEDNESDAY 11 AUGUST

1 Chronicles 16:15–18
'To you I will give the land of Canaan as the portion you will inherit.' (v18)

I look at my life as entrusted into my care by God. I'm responsible, through God's guidance, to use my life, wherever I find myself, to love and serve God, which includes other people (Mark 12:30–31). Each Israeli tribe was given a portion of land to care for, with the majority in the Promised Land; but Reuben, Gad and the half tribe of Manasseh had east of the Jordan (Josh. 13:8). When we surrender to Jesus, God entrusts our new life back into our hands. What shall we do with it?

On reflection, I've frittered many years away. I never rejected God, but I wasn't diligent in pursuit of spiritual formation. I was happy enough to accept God's love, attend church but use the rest of my time pleasing myself. God was at the edge, not the middle, of my life's adventure.

Like many, an unanticipated event shocked me into reflecting on what I was doing with my life. I knew I had to respond to God more intentionally or risked losing hold of Him completely.

At this point I was reminded of the scriptures God had repeatedly impressed upon me in the first three years of my Christian life, and also a significant prophecy I'd studiously ignored. This was the time to take seriously my invitation to cultivate the land given me by God. This meant addressing my own spiritual condition so I might cultivate my inheritance.

RELATED SCRIPTURE TO CONSIDER: Josh. 14:6–15; Psa. 51:10–17; Isa. 55:1–7; Matt. 25:14–30.

AN ACTION TO TAKE: If you have questions over your own Christian growth consider joining our College courses on spiritual formation: **edwj.org/ja21-11aug**

A PRAYER TO MAKE: 'Lord, help me to curate and cultivate the life You have given me and so become the best of who You created me to be. Amen.'

Size Doesn't Matter

1 Chronicles 16:19–24

'When they were but few in number, few indeed, and strangers in it, they wandered from nation to nation, from one kingdom to another.' (v19)

In 1938, with the world on the verge of war, F.D. Roosevelt, President of the USA, paused a cabinet meeting to join an estimated 40 million Americans in listening to commentary on a horse race in Baltimore. The race was the long anticipated run off between the aristocratic and Triple Crown winning War Admiral, and the undersized and underachieving Seabiscuit (pawned off to horse owner Charles Howard for just $8,000 two years earlier). Like Goliath to the diminutive David, War Admiral lost the contest by four lengths, a whopping ten metres.*

There are many voices expressing concern at the decline of the Christian Church. Indeed, the recent UK Census is expected to reveal that those identifying as Christian across the nation will fall below 50% for the first time.** Yet, let's place our confidence in Jesus' words and refuse to worry (John 14:27). God has ensured that from the beginning of time His name has been known. Individuals in search of God found Him and He established a people. They wandered in the desert, were given a homeland and endured captivity. In time, Jesus came to deal with the separation between God and humanity.

Both experience and history reveal that size doesn't matter. God's purpose is unstoppable and we are privileged to participate in it. Do not fear! No act of government, special interest group or national disinterest can prevent God from filling the earth with His glory as the waters cover the sea (Hab. 2:14)

RELATED SCRIPTURE TO CONSIDER: Psa. 78; Hab. 3:16–19; Acts 2:22–41; 28:17–31.

AN ACTION TO TAKE: One thing we must all learn to do is to trust God even in the face of contradictory evidence (2 Cor. 5:7). How challenging do you find that?

A PRAYER TO MAKE: 'Lord, I give thanks that nothing and no one can undermine Your Word of truth. Amen.'

*https://www.theguardian.com/sport/2013/nov/01/seabiscuit-war-admiral-horse-race-1938-pimlico [accessed 21/03/2021]
**https://www.theguardian.com/uk-news/2021/mar/20/less-that-half-of-britons-expected-to-tick-christian-in-uk-census [accessed 21/03/2021]

Become part of someone's testimony

Our Bible reading notes are read by hundreds of thousands of people around the world, and *Every Day with Jesus* and *Inspiring Women Every Day* have recently been made free in the UK. We want everyone, whatever their financial means, to have access to these resources that help them walk each day with our Saviour.

Here's what one *Every Day with Jesus* reader wrote to us:

Ever since I started using Everyday with Jesus, I reconnected to the Lord directly again. It deals with my day to day and minute to minute problems in details. Guiding me in the most solemn and right direction for a dedicated Christian living.

As we trust in God's provision, we know there are costs to providing this ministry. Do you have a passion for God's Word changing lives? Could supporting this vision be a way in which you serve?

A gift of just £2 a month from you will put daily Bible reading notes into the hands of at least one person who is hungry to know God and experience His presence every day.

Visit **waverleyabbeyresources.org/donate** to become part of someone's testimony, or use the form at the back of these notes.

1 Chronicles 16:25–30
'For all the gods of the nations are idols, but the LORD made the heavens.' (v26)

C. S. Lewis identified the central distinction of our age as the difference between true religion and idolatry, not that between secularism and religion.[*] Idolatry comes in many forms – personality cults, wealth accumulation, infatuation, even secularism.

Secularism, properly defined, is 'a system which seeks to interpret and order life on principles taken solely from this world, without recourse to belief in God and a future life'[**] It also proposes 'a closed system that affirms that human existence and destiny are fully explainable in terms of this world without reference to eternity'.[***] Secularism is a form of idolatry seeking to dethrone God and worship human achievement and possibility. Idolatry is to worship the wrong thing in place of God. We have our instructions in the two greatest commandments (Matt: 22:37). Anything directing our gaze away from God, whilst also blinding us to the interests of others (Phil. 2:3), means that we deny God.

Whilst we may want to choose language carefully in a complex world of political correctness, itself subject to interminable battles over the rights of various communities who make up and contribute to society, we must never allow ourselves to deny the reality that God is always above all and in all (Eph. 4:6).

RELATED SCRIPTURE TO CONSIDER: Exod. 20:1–7; Jonah 2:7–10; Rom. 1: 21–25; 1 Cor. 10:12–24.

AN ACTION TO TAKE: Are there activities, ambitions or desires that are focused beyond the way and will of God in your life? Take steps to move towards God and away from these idols that all too easily consume your aspirations and actions.

A PRAYER TO MAKE: 'Lord, strengthen my resolve to live for You and Your will entirely, just as Jesus gave His life entirely for me. Amen.'

[*]https://www.discovery.org/a/510/ [accessed 21/03/2021]
[**]Secularism, Oxford Dictionary of the Christian Church ed. F.L. Cross and E.A. Livingstone, 2nd ed. (Oxford: O.U.P. 1974) p.p. 1255 – 1256.
[***]John A. Hardon S.J. Modern Catholic Dictionary (New York: Doubleday, 1980) ìsecularismî p. 496.

Creation Cries Out

1 Chronicles 16:31–36
'Let the heavens rejoice, let the earth be glad; let them
say among the nations, "The LORD reigns!"' (v31)

Nature is both wonderful and overwhelming. We can sit and
bask in the beauty of a sunset or rush to high ground to avoid a
tsunami. Nature captures the imagination of poets and artists
and is also ruthlessly exploited for commercial gain.

All of this beautiful world of ours was created by God. Whilst
humanity may have been the final piece in God's creation story, it
remains dependent upon nature to sustain life itself. The more we
understand about our planet, the more it seems that there is an
interconnectedness which looks to the wise stewardship of humanity
to ensure its balance is maintained to sustain us all.

Scripture reminds us that creation itself groans in expectation
of Christ's return. Indeed, Isaiah describes the close relationship
between God and His creation (Isa. 55:12–13). We must be careful
never to allow ourselves to become separated from nature for there is
an essential link between every created element within God's world.

We carry a responsibility to proclaim with confidence that 'Our God
reigns'. When silenced by circumstance, fear or government dictat,
creation has no option but to raise its voice instead (Luke 19:40). One
reason perhaps why we encounter the very presence of God in both
the silence of a gentle sunrise and the fury of a cyclonic storm.

RELATED SCRIPTURE TO CONSIDER: Psa. 19:1–9; Amos 9:5–6; Rom. 1:16–20; 8:18–27.

AN ACTION TO TAKE: Take time to go for a walk and consider the God who
created all that you see.

A PRAYER TO MAKE: 'Lord, thank You for the fullness and interconnectedness of
Your creation. May we treat this gift with respect. Amen.'

1 Chronicles 16:37–43
**'Then all the people left, each for their own home, and
David returned home to bless his family.'** (v43)

Worship is neither a location nor a specific time. Just as Zadok the priest continued to sacrifice before God's tabernacle, so we're invited to worship 24/7. We now carry God's tabernacle within us, so no matter where we go we are always able to worship.

As temples of the Holy Spirit, we are perpetually in God's presence and everything we do becomes an act of worship (1 Cor. 6:19–20). Whilst we may select times to gather as congregations, this is only one form of worship. It is not the only worship we are invited to give God. Good news for many who through disability, illness or other circumstances can never attend a physical Christian gathering.

I also draw comfort because as I grow older, less mobile and inevitably lose friends to eternity, I will never be in a position where I cannot worship God. Like all things I believe this takes some consistent practice so that, when required, I shall find myself reaching out to God rather than consumed with my own loneliness.

Already I am reaping the benefit from establishing a rhythm of worshipful pauses through my day, as described this week. For I know that I'll encounter God in the silence and solitude wherever I am. If I fail to carry my worship with me wherever I find myself, then I must revisit my whole approach to worship.

RELATED SCRIPTURE TO CONSIDER: 1 Kings 8:27–30; Psa. 139: 7–12; John 4:19–24; Acts 16:22–34.

AN ACTION TO TAKE: Make a plan to strengthen your worship muscle through dedicated practice in worshipping God as frequently as you can.

A PRAYER TO MAKE: 'Lord, I give You thanks that nothing can separate me from Your love, for I am always in Your presence. Amen' (Rom. 8:38–39).

Psalm 130:5–8

'I wait for the LORD, my whole being waits, and in his word I put my hope.' (v5)

An ambassador's role and we are all appointed God's ambassadors is waiting. Choosing the ideal moment for intervention, as well as the nature of that intervention, always proves critical (2 Cor. 5:20). The context in which we are to present the gospel is subject to continual change. As Billy Graham stated, we are always to be geared to the times, whilst anchored to the rock.* Scripture records that the men of Issachar were 'men who understood the times and knew what Israel should do' (1 Chron. 12:32), a useful gift for any ambassador.

It's challenging standing firm on God's truth, whilst navigating fast-changing social mores. If we simply rely on a traditional framework to communicate God's truth, like a sandcastle before an incoming tide, we will be washed away. It's not that we abandon God's eternal, Bible truth, but that we reframe it so that we can be both heard and understood within the prevailing culture to which God has sent us as witnesses.

Too often the Christian community surrenders ground unnecessarily because it fails to understand both the battlefield and the nature of the battle it is engaged in. David could not defeat Goliath wearing Saul's armour, but did by utilising his learned skills, demonstrating that Yahweh is Lord of all.

RELATED SCRIPTURE TO CONSIDER: Isa. 43:10–13; Acts 3:15–20; 5:29–42; 17:16–31.

AN ACTION TO TAKE: Take some time to consider how you can present God's eternal truth in ways that connect with contemporary society in general and your peer group in particular.

A PRAYER TO MAKE: 'Lord, train me to be one who understands the times and can communicate as a witness anchored to the rock whilst still geared to the times. Amen.'

*https://fromthevault.wheaton.edu/2019/11/02/still-geared-to-the-times-anchored-to-the-rock-seventy-five-years-of-youth-for-christ/ [accessed 21/03/2021]

Spirit-Led

Romans 8:12–17
**'The Spirit himself testifies with our spirit
that we are God's children.'** (v16)

The word 'flesh' occurs 147 times in the New Testament, 97 of which are in Paul's letters (principally Romans and Galatians). Flesh is not of itself evil, but rather transient. Life 'in the flesh' is normal human existence, yet is still only human (Gal 2:20). The same meaning is found in the Old Testament. Since our humanity is sin's gateway, and often the vehicle by which sin is practised, it can only lead us towards death (Rom. 8:6–8).

The Spirit, however, is the deposit on our inheritance in Christ (Eph. 1:14). As disciples, we are invited to live by the Spirit, not the flesh. He enables us to engage with God, which the flesh can't do. Therefore we are invited to live by the Spirit, in touch with eternity whilst still rooted on the earth (Phil. 3:3). The flesh, always subject to temptation, has the capacity to lead us away from God, and Jesus warned His disciples that it is always in conflict with God's Spirit (Mark 14:38).

Our challenge is to enjoy the fruits of the freedom won for us on the cross. It is to find ways to choose the life of the Spirit that is, the life available to us in Christ rather than our life course being subject to the flesh. As God's ambassadors, learning to live as agents for God's kingdom will require both our vigilance and personal discipline.

RELATED SCRIPTURE TO CONSIDER: Psa. 104:27–30; Ezek. 37:1–14; Gal. 5:13–26; Eph. 1:15–23.

AN ACTION TO TAKE: Our Christian understanding comes from the Bible. Search the Scriptures offers an easy to use, three-year, personal study guide to the Bible. A worthwhile investment for every disciple: Pick up your copy at **edwj.org/ja21-17aug**

A PRAYER TO MAKE: 'Lord, help me to choose Spirit over flesh and so learn to live in step with the Spirit of God. Amen.'

2 Corinthians 10:1–5

'The weapons we fight with are not the weapons of the world. On the contrary, they have divine power to demolish strongholds.' (v4)

I was once asked if it was possible to be both a pacifist and a Christian. I thought for a moment and replied, 'No! But maybe not in the way you might think.'

My dad experienced the horrors of fighting a physical war for his country from 1939 to 1946. He spoke little of his experiences, but did make me promise I'd never join the armed forces. Warfare had opened his eyes to the horrors it unleashes.

Scripture is clear that if we follow Jesus we are by default engaging in warfare. This is in the form of a resistance movement in resisting Satan from exercising his dominion on earth. He does this through appealing to the desires of our flesh, and in so doing maintains, and increases, our separation from God (1 Pet. 5:8–9).

Our responsibility is to live and demonstrate that the practical reality of God's kingdom mandate is possible for every Spirit-filled Christian. To do so, we must be sure to get a measure of both our enemy and the tactics that will be used against us. Much of this is driven by unseen forces that seek to invade our thoughts and direct our actions. Making those thoughts our prisoner at the earliest opportunity disempowers them, and empowers us to choose for God within life's countless pressures.

RELATED SCRIPTURE TO CONSIDER: Psa. 91; Isa. 54:9–17; Rom. 8:31–39; 2 Thess. 3:1–5.

AN ACTION TO TAKE: Take time learning to understand your thought patterns so you can discover how to interrupt and take captive negative thoughts, and those that tempt you to sin.

A PRAYER TO MAKE: 'Lord, You are my rock and I take refuge in You. When in trouble I choose to call out to You for help. Amen' (cf Psa. 18:1–3).

John 3:16–21

'For God did not send his Son into the world to condemn the world, but to save the world through him.' (v17)

The Church easily adopts a 'siege mentality', a defensive or paranoid attitude based on the belief that others are hostile towards it. Throughout my Christian life, many prophecies from various Christian communities have offered dire warnings and catastrophic predictions.

As ambassadors, God invites us to represent the best of God's interests here on earth. Jesus, whose ministry was consistently contested and whose life was taken by force, came with a message of hope. God moved out of love, despite the violent consequences such love provoked. It should come as no surprise that God's message of eternal love through personal surrender can stir up extreme reaction.

God's proposition is that love expressed towards both God and neighbour is sufficient to provoke a response (Mark 12:30–31). Yet, the response may still be negative. Over 260 million Christians, across 78 countries, daily face persecution for their faith, one reason we're associate members of the Religious Liberty Partnership (rlpartnership.org) and make *EDWJ* freely available digitally.

Adolf Hitler stated, 'To conquer a nation, first disarm its citizens'. God came in search of His citizens and armed them with a love that transcends all obstacles so that everyone might discover 'how wide and long and high and deep is the love of Christ' (Eph. 3:18).

RELATED SCRIPTURE TO CONSIDER: Jer. 31:1–6; Jonah 3:6–4:4; 1 John 4:7–21; Jude 1.

AN ACTION TO TAKE: Learning to love can prove challenging. Yet, God's salvation message was born in love, and is only communicated through love, a love that reveals the conflict between light and darkness. Are you able to love, whilst living in the light, so that darkness is exposed?

A PRAYER TO MAKE: 'Lord, help me to reveal God's love and invite others to journey from darkness into the wonderful light of Your salvation. Amen.'

2 Corinthians 5:15–21
'God was reconciling the world to himself in Christ, not counting people's sins against them. And he has committed to us the message of reconciliation.' (v19)

A worldly view is best described as living for one's own self-interest, most often pursued without regard for others. This is the complete opposite to living for Christ and contradicts God's Word.

We're invited, as God's ambassadors, to view everyone through the lens of God's kingdom interest. It may take work but I'm to look beyond where I find fault in another, stop my criticism (which will only bring both of us down) and learn to see them as Christ does. He regards no one from a human point of view (v16).

Since God came in search of humanity when there was no one who was godly, I don't enjoy the luxury of viewing Christians any differently from those who as yet have failed to encounter God and salvation. If I do, I simply judge myself (John 8:15).

The act of reconciliation can only begin when those in conflict with each other meet, albeit with a mediator present to manage their process. I have worked as a professional mediator for over 20 years and have learnt, whatever my preconceptions, to never say never. The most apparently intractable problems have a path to resolution. As God's agents, we are required to work to encourage such reconciliation as witnesses to God's salvation.

RELATED SCRIPTURE TO CONSIDER: Psa. 85; Isa. 64:5–12; Rom. 5:6–11; Eph. 2.

AN ACTION TO TAKE: Do you find yourself criticising others, whilst failing to see your own faults? Take practical steps to acknowledge and cut short this criticism and pray for their wellbeing instead.

A PRAYER TO MAKE: 'Lord, I offer myself to be a peacemaker in our conflicted world, one inspired and guided by Your Spirit. Amen.'

Write to **micha@edwj.org** and I'll write back personally and in confidence as soon as I can.

No Limits

Ephesians 6:18–20
'for which [the gospel] I am an ambassador in chains. Pray that I may declare it fearlessly, as I should.' (v20)

In surrendering to Christ, we discover there are no limits beyond which God refuses to lead us. Scripture says that wherever we find ourselves, it is for the proclamation of the gospel; perhaps with few words and by our physical testimony to faithfulness.

Just as the Bible tells us that the leopard can't change its spots, so we are encouraged to remain devoted and dependable in all circumstances (Jer. 13:23). Of course, Scripture states that God will not test us beyond what we can endure, yet in advance of any trial we don't know where that point might be (1 Cor. 10:13).

Paul remains God's ambassador, albeit in chains. These are the physical chains that hold him captive. Yet, we must wrestle with many invisible chains that can equally restrict our freedom. Our temptation is always to yield to pressure, for the immediate relief that follows feels comforting, however short lived.

Such surrender may leave our Christian confession compromised. Whilst there's always a way back through repentance, there will be consequences that can weaken our witness in the eyes of others. This is why Paul reminds us to pray all the time, whilst keeping our eyes open for possible compromises before they overtake us. As we pray for ourselves, let's also pray for each other, for we are on this journey together, never alone.

RELATED SCRIPTURE TO CONSIDER: 1 Sam. 17:41–47; Isa. 41:11–16; Jam. 1:2–18; 1 Pet. 5:1–11.

AN ACTION TO TAKE: Fear is often a far larger barrier than the thing that gives rise to fear. Scripture says many times, 'fear not'. Talk through your fears with God and determine the limits you might have in following Jesus.

A PRAYER TO MAKE: 'Lord, help me to own and then entrust my deepest fears to You, knowing You promise to always accompany me. Amen.'

Proverbs 13:10–20
**'A wicked messenger falls into trouble, but a
trustworthy envoy brings healing.'** (v17)

The word 'wicked' entered into the English language around 1200.*
An adjective from wicca, the Old English for 'wizard', it meant
'bad or false'. Bad means unsatisfactory, whilst false means lying
intentionally. In Christian usage, it meant someone who was not of the
Christian faith.

These are obviously adjectives we do not want to describe us. We
can, of course, pull the wool over people's eyes, itself an idiom for
deceit and untruth, but the deposit we leave in relationships and
situations is dis-ease. In other words, we prevent things functioning
as they should; preventing success and doing harm.

It's why truth is essential for trust building, for without trust there
is no confidence and little can be achieved. Whilst we see so many
apparent successes built upon what later proves to be a corrupt
foundation, God is to be trusted. His Word is forever trustworthy.

Our model is Jesus, who knew when to keep silent and, when He
did speak, reiterated the foundational truths upon which the good,
or God, life might be confidently established and built. As God's
ambassadors, we must remain above reproach. Where we make
mistakes, we are to be swift to acknowledge them to all who have
suffered as a consequence.

Truth telling is an act of the will and a way of life; it constructs the
paving stones for God's way.

RELATED SCRIPTURE TO CONSIDER: Psa. 15; Luke 16:1-14; 1 Pet. 3:8-18; 1 John 1:5-7.

AN ACTION TO TAKE: Are you trustworthy? What can you do to build trust both
within and outside the church?

A PRAYER TO MAKE: 'Lord, I choose to be transparent with You and seek advice
and support where I struggle with my Christian witness. Amen.'

*https://www.etymonline.com/word/wicked [accessed 21/03/2021]

1 Corinthians 11:17-32
**'Everyone ought to examine themselves before they
eat of the bread and drink from the cup.'** (v28)

Criticism cuts deep. A group of people whose loving community
is to provide tangible evidence of the truth of the gospel, often
falters in its execution (John 13:35). The Communion table
demands that we ensure our conscience is clear and our relationship
issues have been addressed. Jesus says we must press pause on
taking Communion if someone has a problem with us (Matt. 5:23-24).
God leaves no room for broken relationships.

Taking Communion provokes us to manage our relationships, so
it's sad this isn't a weekly event in all churches. Paul knows the
foundational value of community. Snapshots of the first Christians
present a picture of cohesion and mutuality. Many of us long for such
a community, but recognise it will exact a price. We cannot have
community on our terms.

Sadly, following separation from Rome at the Reformation, the
church has yet to find the capacity to stop splintering. The Center
for the Study of Global Christianity at Gordon–Conwell Theological
Seminary estimated 43,000 independent Christian groups in 2012,
rising from 1,600 in 1900.*

There may be legitimate reasons, but the optics don't look good.
As part of our ministry of reconciliation, we must work better together
and reflect the foundational message of the Christian Church
(Matt. 28:17-20).

RELATED SCRIPTURE TO CONSIDER: Mal. 2:1-16; Matt. 18:21-35;
Acts 2:42-47; 4:32-35.

AN ACTION TO TAKE: What do you feel about building community as an
expression of God's commitment to draw all people to Himself (John 12:32)?
Where can you start?

A PRAYER TO MAKE: 'Lord, help me to honour You within my relationships and
work to encourage community across the Church. Amen.'

*https://www.gordonconwell.edu/center-for-global-christianity/ [accessed 21/03/2021]

2 Corinthians 3:17-18
**'Now the LORD is the Spirit, and where the Spirit
of the LORD is, there is freedom.'** (v17)

The purpose of spiritual formation is personal transformation. This is evident by marked changes. Many tell of a significant change at conversion, but transformation is a process, never an event. If my life's testimony is only my conversion story, then maybe I'm in need of an update.

Our garden is frequented by snails. We can see their trails where they've crisscrossed our patio. Looking back, we should see clear progress in our Christian life stretching behind us like a snail trail. If there is no trail, then my journey may have stagnated.

As disciples, we're never in competition with each other, for we each have a distinct purpose entrusted to us by God. Nor do two journeys look the same. God walks alongside us, interpreting the Scriptures to reveal more of Himself. When we stagnate, we stop growing and, once we stop growing spiritually, our faith starts dying. Many pull out of their faith journey part way through. They lose sight of God and dismiss much of what they once believed.

This can happen to any of us. Hence our need to keep seeking transformation by daily looking to God. One way to do this is with *EDWJ*, but there are other elements we can add to empower us in this journey of spiritual formation. It's our responsibility to pursue transformation; it doesn't come looking for us.

RELATED SCRIPTURE TO CONSIDER: Psa. 103:1-5; Lam. 3:19-27; 2 Pet. 1:3-11; 1 John 3:1-6.

AN ACTION TO TAKE: What is your testimony of transformation? Where do you see God at work in your life and what are you actively seeking in God?

A PRAYER TO MAKE: 'Lord, guide my steps daily so I discover more of You and learn how to fulfil Your purpose in my life. Amen.'

Romans 1:16-17

'For I am not ashamed of the gospel, because it is the power of God that brings salvation to everyone who believes: first to the Jew, then to the Gentile.' (v16)

The gospel means 'good story', and we all like a good story. It's why TV streaming services have boomed. Daily we witness, just like Paul, good news stories of Jesus at work in our lives.

Sadly, the gospel is often reduced to a proposition. It can sound like a psychological theory. Jesus, Himself the good news, didn't lecture on metaphysics. He ate dinners with people, spoke at open air picnics and provided the wine to at least one wedding, something that's always appreciated.

We all have favourite biblical texts and 'sound' theological convictions, but these are never welcome at the neighbourhood barbecue. Better to tell stories about where and how God makes sense in everyday life, for we all share similar life experiences.

When the radiator partially fell off the wall, strained a joint and I watched water spraying into the living room, my state of shock was interrupted by the doorbell. A quick arrow prayer and I opened the door to my neighbour. I explained that it may not be a good moment, but he announced that his dad, a plumber, was visiting. In an hour, the problem was resolved. Good news indeed! Coincidence or God-incidence well, it's left to the reader's discretion. Witnessing is sharing good stories about how God makes sense in our everyday lives.

RELATED SCRIPTURE TO CONSIDER: 2 Kings 4:1–7; Isa. 12; Acts 4:8–17; 1 John 1:1–4.

AN ACTION TO TAKE: What good stories can you tell where you have encountered God in everyday life? Who can you share them with, and when?

A PRAYER TO MAKE: 'Lord, open my eyes to the encounters I have with You in my daily life so that I have good stories to tell to those I meet every day. Amen.'

Rejoice in the Lord Always

September introduces the autumn in Northern Europe. Traditionally a time of giving thanks, for the harvest is gathered in. Significant because it not only guarantees food for the long, cold winter ahead, but gives the seed for replanting in Spring. Seasons may change around the world, but God invites us all to give thanks for God's provision, from our basic needs to those special moments that warm our hearts. In the next issue we will look at why, how and for what purpose we give thanks to God, even when our own lives might be passing through a bleak winter season.

Also available as esubscription, ebook, audioversion and PDF.

Obtain your copy from **waverleyabbeyresources.org** or a Christian bookshop

Galatians 2:20–21
'I have been crucified with Christ and I no longer live, but Christ lives in me. The life I now live in the body, I live by faith in the Son of God, who loved me and gave himself for me.' (v20)

I struggled at school, always feeling disengaged in the classroom. Quickly bored, my mind yearned to explore things I was interested in. When priorities are set for us, we can quickly lose focus, grow frustrated and become demotivated. So spiritual formation is only fruitful when it's our choice and not something expected of us. It must be our chosen priority.

A priority is something of first importance in our lives. As disciples, we choose to put God's interests first (John 3:30). In busy lives it's easy to miss our priorities or is it? Actually, there are many things we successfully achieve every day; these prove to be our true priorities. Whilst priority lists capture what needs to be done, what actually gets done reveals our true priority. Paul had no doubts; Christ came first. Reading his life story in Scripture supports his declaration. What priorities does my life reveal? Bonhoeffer wrote: 'The cross is laid on every Christian. The first Christ-suffering which every man must experience is the call to abandon the attachments of this world. It is that dying of the old man which is the result of his encounter with Christ.'*

Sounds intense! But once we make spiritual formation our #1 priority, it brings order and purpose to our daily life, informs our choices and creates great peace of mind. Gone are the struggles with thoughts such as 'I should' and 'I ought', replaced with a simple 'I will'.

RELATED SCRIPTURE TO CONSIDER: Luke 9:23–36; John 12:24–26; Eph. 4:17–24; Phil. 3:7–14.

AN ACTION TO TAKE: Bonhoeffer also wrote: 'Discipleship is not an offer that man makes to Christ'. God has called you; how does that influence your primary priority in life?

A PRAYER TO MAKE: 'Lord, help me to deny myself, take up my cross daily and follow You entirely. Amen.'

*Dietrich Bonhoeffer *The Cost of Discipleship* (New York: SCM, 1966)

Acts 17:22–34
**'For as I walked around and looked carefully at your objects
of worship, I even found an altar with this inscription: to
an unknown god. So you are ignorant of the very thing you
worship – and this is what I am going to proclaim to you.'** (v23)

Agility is the ability to adapt quickly to change. Those who built
America's railroads failed to see they were creating a mass
transport system. Their focus on railways alone meant they
failed to grasp the opportunities for roads that motor vehicles
offered, and later air travel. Those railways today largely transport
freight, not people.

Paul, sees an inscription and seizes on it to present the 'God who
made the world and everything in it'. Our challenge is always to retain
the agility to engage with our changing context. My daughter loved
our family celebration of Thanksgiving. All her friends wanted to come,
eat and participate in a meal during which we gave thanks to God
and identified something to ask of God in prayer for the year ahead.
Recorded in a book, we returned each Thanksgiving to review and
discover how God had answered our prayers.

Many conversations started with these young people, none of
whom was willing to visit a church youth group. Agility requires our
willingness to take a risk. Athens was the intellectual centre of the
contemporary world, where Christian ideas were required to shift the
rational resistance to Christian truth. We need to find creative ways to
challenge unbelief once again in our own society.

RELATED SCRIPTURE TO CONSIDER: Neh. 2:1–9; Dan. 1:8–20; Luke 19:11–27;
2 Tim. 4:1–4.

AN ACTION TO TAKE: Do you observe life through the rearview mirror, rooted in
where you have come from, or through the windscreen at where you are
headed? Make sure you look through the windscreen so you are prepared to
take whatever action the road ahead requires.

A PRAYER TO MAKE: 'Lord, give me the courage and ability to think and move
swiftly in response to the opportunities the Spirit offers. Amen.'

Ephesians 5:15–21

'speaking to one another with psalms, hymns, and songs from the Spirit. Sing and make music from your heart to the Lord,' (v19)

Life challenges us with a multitude of responsibilities, amongst which we barely find time to draw breath. It's healthy to build in moments of thanksgiving throughout our day. Such moments will ground us and remind us of the good things that life offers us – children, fine food and friendships, for example.

Thanksgiving is the bass note for God's constant communication with us because the bass plays a powerful role in how we hear harmonies. When we hear several notes played at the same time, we hear them all relative to the lowest sounding pitch — the bass note. It stands out by virtue of being an outer voice. It's what helps us distinguish between music and noise. Being below all the others, the bass note gives the impression of supporting them all. Thanksgiving does the same.

A noisy world, constantly demanding our attention, produces a noisy mind. Our thoughts are filled with never-ending demands that quickly build stress throughout our whole being. A moment to pause and give thanks is our opportunity to draw near to God and find rest for ourselves (Matt. 11:28).

A world in persistent pursuit of wellbeing needs help regulating its life's rhythm with moments of thanksgiving – thanks for God's presence, friends and family, and a knowledge that God accepts and loves it (Psa. 46:10).

RELATED SCRIPTURE TO CONSIDER: Psa. 100; Isa. 41:1–10; Phil. 4:4–9; Col. 3:15–17.

AN ACTION TO TAKE: Consider your average day and identify moments of praise you can add in. Make it a habit to pause and give thanks, regardless of how you feel, at each one of these moments.

A PRAYER TO MAKE: 'Lord, thank You that You are good and Your love endures forever. I will praise You throughout my day. Amen' (1 Chron. 16:34).

Isaiah 43:1–2
**'Do not fear, for I have redeemed you; I have
summoned you by name; you are mine'** (v1b)

There are many pressures each of us faces daily. Yet, we are
reassured that God is always with us. This is because He has laid
down His life in Jesus in exchange for the release of each of us
from the bondage of sin. Much like Israel experienced slavery under
the Egyptians (Exod. 1:8–14), so humanity has been held captive by
Satan since the Fall (Gen. 3). Just as God led Israel to freedom through
the Red Sea, so we, by accepting the death and resurrection of Jesus,
can be freed from sin and death. Baptism symbolises our crossing
of the Red Sea, moving from slavery to freedom and inheriting all the
promises of God.

Slavery is like an addiction; despite our best intentions we are
controlled by forces beyond our control (Rom. 7:15). The good news
is that not only has God redeemed us, but He calls us by name. We
can choose to ignore God's voice, or we can pay heed and respond.
Every journey with God is dormant until the individual called says yes
(John 1:35–39).

From this point on our friendship with God can deepen day by day.
But it remains dependent upon our continued desire to follow and
find out more about Jesus. Reassuringly, God never tires of us and
will never walk away since He has made us heirs with Christ. God can
never give up on us.

RELATED SCRIPTURE TO CONSIDER: Rom. 6:1–14; 7:7–8:17.

AN ACTION TO TAKE: Ask yourself: have you found freedom from sin by
surrendering to Jesus? Have you chosen to respond to Jesus' call, 'Come
follow me?' Do you encounter Jesus daily in your regular life?

A PRAYER TO MAKE: 'Lord, hear my decision: 'I have decided to follow Jesus, the
world behind me, the cross before me, though none go with me I will follow,
my cross I'll carry till I see Jesus''. Help me to live this prayer every day.
Amen.'

'Attributed to S. Sundar Singh, library.timelesstruths.org/music/I_Have_Decided_to_Follow_Jesus

I Am With You

Colossians. 4:2–6
**'Be wise in the way you act towards outsiders;
make the most of every opportunity.'** (v5)

Over two months, we've looked long and hard at our responsibilities as God's ambassadors (2 Cor. 5:20). Paul here lays the foundations for all God's ambassadors; prayer and witness.

Disciples serve as God's visible and tangible expression on earth. How we face challenges, handle relationships, establish boundaries and treat others all reveal the values we've adopted. Indeed, the first view anybody gets of Christianity is their observation of its followers.

The Christian community can easily defend itself against criticism, but when it does will it make friends or confirm suspicions? It might be wise to pause and listen. Of course, some criticism is unwarranted and intended to damage the Christian claim. However, much of it is worth listening to since it reflects individuals' experience of the Church.

While leading a church for 18 years I always talked to visitors. Their most common criticism was that the church was unfriendly. During times of meet and greet over coffee, the committed church members studiously ignored newcomers and invested in their existing relationships. Having visited lively churches myself, I have endured the same experience.

Treating criticism with respect will prove the most effective way both to inform our prayers and instruct us in how best to act towards outsiders as God's ambassadors.

RELATED SCRIPTURE TO CONSIDER: Prov: 18:1–17; Matt. 5:43–48; Eph. 5:15–20; 1 Pet. 4:9–17.

AN ACTION TO TAKE: God has given us two ears, but only one mouth. Time to listen twice as much as we speak. Learn to ask questions and listen to what others are saying. How does that impact your understanding?

A PRAYER TO MAKE: 'Lord, encourage me to pray for others, listen to others and serve others. Amen.'

Titus 2:11–15
**'It teaches us to say "No" to ungodliness and
worldly passions, and to live self-controlled, upright
and godly lives in this present age'** (v12)

Each of us is chosen by God and appointed as His ambassador. It is a responsibility that we are equipped for by God's Holy Spirit. Although daunting, like Joshua and Jericho, we are invited to see the opportunity despite the challenge (Num. 13:27–30).

Every ambassador continually learns on the job. Their responsibility is to represent their country well and appropriately in a foreign land. We are citizens of heaven, and are invited to represent God's promises to those we serve, for we have no citizenship rights where we serve (Heb. 13:14).

We might view our church as our embassy, filled with those like us seeking to represent God's kingdom. And we may feel homesick on occasion, yearning simply to be with the Lord. However, our task is always before us, making known the goodness of God in the land of the living (Psa. 27:13). It is a wonderful commission direct from God.

Tomorrow, as we begin a fresh adventure exploring the height and depth of God's love, for which we are eternally grateful, let's faithfully pursue our responsibility to continue faithfully as God's ambassadors. We pray and work so that 'the earth will be filled with the knowledge of the glory of the LORD as the waters cover the sea' (Hab. 2:14).

RELATED SCRIPTURE TO CONSIDER: Isa. 6:1–8; Luke 6:27–36; 2 Tim. 1:6–14; Heb. 13:1–18.

AN ACTION TO TAKE: Make some time to reflect on your ambassadorial role, and how you can continue to discover more about how to serve God more effectively in the years ahead.

A PRAYER TO MAKE: 'Lord, thank You that You have appointed me as Your ambassador and continue to equip me for this responsibility of serving You in every sphere of my life. Amen.'

Write to **micha@edwj.org** and I'll write back personally and in confidence as soon as I can.

Notes

Order form

Get Your **FREE** Daily Bible Reading Notes **TODAY!** (UK ONLY)

Your favourite Bible Reading notes are now available to you for FREE. God has called us back to the original vision of CWR to provide these notes to everyone who needs them, regardless of their circumstance or ability to pay. It is our desire to see these daily Bible reading notes used more widely, to see Christians grow in their relationship with Jesus on a daily basis and to see Him reflected in their everyday living. Clearly there are costs to provide this ministry and we are trusting in God's provision.

Could you be part of this vision? Do you have the desire to see lives transformed through a relationship with Jesus? **A small donation from you of just £2 a month, by direct debit, will make such a difference** Giving hope to someone in desperate need whilst you too grow deeper in your own relationship with Jesus.

4 Easy Ways To Order

1. Visit our online store at **waverleyabbeyresources.org/store**
2. Send this form together with your payment to:
   CWR, Waverley Abbey House, Waverley Lane, Farnham, Surrey GU9 8EP
3. Phone in your credit card order: **01252 784700** (Mon–Fri, 9.30am – 4.30pm)
4. Visit a Christian bookshop

For a list of our National Distributors, who supply countries outside the UK, visit waverleyabbeyresources.org/distributors

Your **Details** (required for orders and donations)

Full Name:

CWR ID No. (if known):

Home Address:

Postcode:

Telephone No. (for queries):

Email:

Publications

TITLE	QTY	PRICE	TOTAL
		Total Publications	

UK P&P: up to £24.99 = **£2.99**; £25.00 and over = **FREE**

Elsewhere P&P: up to £10 = **£4.95**; £10.01 – £50 = **£6.95**; £50.01 – £99.99 = **£10**; £100 and over = **£30**

Total Publications and P&P (please allow 14 days for delivery)	**A**	

Payment Details

☐ I enclose a cheque made payable to CWR for the amount of: **£**

☐ Please charge my credit/debit card.

Cardholder's Name (in BLOCK CAPITALS)

Card No. ☐☐☐☐ ☐☐☐☐ ☐☐☐☐ ☐☐☐☐ ☐☐☐☐

Expires End ☐☐ ☐☐   Security Code ☐☐☐

Continued overleaf >>

One off Special Gift to CWR ☐ Please send me an acknowledgement of my gift **B**

GRAND TOTAL (Total of A & B)

Gift Aid (your home address required, see overleaf)

giftaid it I am a UK taxpayer and want CWR to reclaim the tax on all my donations for the four years prior to this year **and on** all donations I make from the date of this Gift Aid declaration until further notice.*

Taxpayer's Full Name (in BLOCK CAPITALS) _____

Signature _____ **Date** _____

*I am a UK taxpayer and understand that if I pay less Income Tax and/or Capital Gains Tax than the amount of Gift Aid claimed on all my donations in that tax year it is my responsibility to pay any difference.

Your FREE Daily Bible Reading Notes Order

	Please Tick	FREE	£2 pcm	£5 pcm	£10 pcm	Other
Every Day with Jesus (1yr, 6 issues)		☐	☐	☐	☐	☐ £ _____
Large Print *Every Day with Jesus* (1yr, 6 issues)		☐	☐	☐	☐	☐ £ _____
Inspiring Women Every Day (1yr, 6 issues)		☐	☐	☐	☐	☐ £ _____

All CWR Bible reading notes are also available in single issue **ebook** and **email subscription** format. Visit **waverleyabbeyresources.org** for further info

---

CWR Instruction to your Bank or Building Society to pay by Direct Debit

Please fill in the form and send to: CWR, Waverley Abbey House, Waverley Lane, Farnham, Surrey GU9 8EP

DIRECT Debit

Name and full postal address of your Bank or Building Society

To: The Manager _____ Bank/Building Society

Address _____

_____ Postcode

Name(s) of Account Holder(s)

Branch Sort Code

Bank/Building Society Account Number

Originator's Identification Number

4	2	0	4	8	7

Reference

Instruction to your Bank or Building Society

Please pay CWR Direct Debits from the account detailed in this Instruction subject to the safeguards assured by the Direct Debit Guarantee. I understand that this Instruction may remain with CWR and, if so, details will be passed electronically to my Bank/Building Society.

Signature(s)

Date

Banks and Building Societies may not accept Direct Debit Instructions for some types of account

---

For a subscription outside of the UK please visit www.waverleyabbeyresources.or where you will find a list of our national distributors.

How would you like to hear from us? We would love to keep you up to date on all aspects of the CWR ministry, including; new publications, events & courses as well as how you can support us.

If you **DO** want to hear from us on email, please tick here [ ] If you **DO NOT** want us to contact you by post, please tick here